CULTURE CLASH

LIFE, DEATH AND REVOLUTIONARY COMEDY

CULTURE CLASH

LIFE, DEATH AND REVOLUTIONARY COMEDY

RICHARD MONTOYA, RICARDO SALINAS, HERBERT SIGUENZA

THE MISSION · A BOWL OF BEINGS · RADIO MAMBO

THEATRE COMMUNICATIONS GROUP

Culture Clash: Life, Death and Revolutionary Comedy is published by
Theatre Communications Group, Inc., 355 Lexington Ave., New York, NY 10017-0217.

This publication is made possible in part with public funds from the New York State
Council on the Arts, a State Agency.

Lalo Guerrero's song "No Chicanos on TV" on pages 39–41 and the excerpt from
Richard Talavera's play *Trial of los Siete* on pages 31–32 are reprinted with permission.

Library of Congress Cataloging-in-Publication Data
Montoya, Richard.
    Culture Clash : life, death and revolutionary comedy / Richard Montoya, Ric Salinas,
and Herbert Siguenza
    The mission—A bowl of beings—Radio mambo.
    ISBN 1-55936-139-5 (alk. paper)
    1. Hispanic Americans—Drama. I. Salinas, Ric. II. Siguenza, Herbert. III. Culture Clash
(comedy troupe) IV. Title.
PS3563.05459C85 1998
812'.54—dc21   97-40168
                                                                                                        CIP

The Mission photos by Eric Riel
A Bowl of Beings photos by Craig Schwartz
Radio Mambo: Culture Clash Invades Miami photos by Ken Jacques
Cover painting by Ignacio Gomez
Cover and book design by Lisa Govan

First Printing, May 1998

For José Antonio Burciaga

CONTENTS

CHICANO IS A STATE OF MIND:
AN INTERVIEW WITH CULTURE CLASH

by Philip Kan Gotanda

The thing about the guys in Culture Clash—and there are a lot of things I could say, though most not publicly—is that they have a "realness" about them. One feels an authenticity about their performances—the content, the style of presentation, the guys themselves. They are not six degrees away but right here, of the moment, inside the tube of contemporary, late twentieth-century, racialized America.

They hold the mirror, albeit tilted at times, to show us who we are right now. These aren't museum pieces they are giving us, made from yesterday's Eurocentric aestheticisms. Rather, their work is living cloth they are continually reinventing as they pull from the threads of social fracture and cultural schism that is the world we live in.

And Culture Clash is fearless at doing what they do. They'll bite the hand that feeds them; they'll bite the hand that spanks them. Hell, they'll bite themselves. Left, right, centrist politics; feminism, male-ism, homophobism; sacred cultural dogmas, traditional biases of every color and persuasion—they're all fair game to get "culture clashed."

They are the second generation of Chicano-Latino theatre artists, inheritors of the political-cultural scene that came out of

'60s activism. They've taken the torch and carried it far and beyond their roots of Teatro Campesino, Salvadorean circuses, the fertile soil of the San Joaquin Valley and the environs of the San Francisco Mission District. They fit into the American theatre terrain along with Anna Deavere Smith, Tony Kushner, David Henry Hwang, George C. Wolfe and others who are giving us new eyes to see who and what we are.

The following interview, plays and accompanying introductions will give you a good sense of what Culture Clash—Herbert Siguenza, Richard Montoya and Ricardo Salinas—is about. I wholeheartedly urge you to read and enjoy, and then read some more. But as one who has seen them from their earliest days to their most recent performances, I encourage you to see them live. Like a good band, they're best experienced from the front row. Disciplined anarchy, performance chaos—it's Culture Clash amped up and alive that is best.

Philip Kan Gotanda
January 1998
Los Angeles, California

PHILIP KAN GOTANDA: How did you originally get together?

HERBERT SIGUENZA: Well, individually, we were all doing theatre in Northern California. And at the time René Yañez, who was the curator of the Galeria de la Raza, was doing some real innovative stuff. Like introducing Frida Kahlo to audiences, bringing groups from L.A. like . . .

RIC SALINAS: ASCO [performance group], and the punk bands from L.A. He was bringing that sensibility up to San Francisco . . .

PHILIP: What year was this?

HERBERT: This would be '82 or so when he was bringing up those L.A. elements, which were really urban and real hip for San Francisco, which was really laid back.

RICHARD MONTOYA: Yeah, there was a performance art scene going on south of Market, SOMA, which was kind of having its hey-day at the time. And René was coming out of that. Culture

Clash was born a couple of years later at Galeria de la Raza/Studio 24. We were kinda out there pushing the envelope as far as performance, theatre, performance art, poetry, music. But I think one thing lacking from that whole scene was humor, and that's always been a big tool of ours, in our theatre and in our songs and in our literature. Even in Chicano literature, there is a humor that goes back to a very Mexican sensibility of life and death and irony. That was lacking in the performing arts scene. And I think it was a conscious decision for René to pull a few people together and say, "Let's do an all-out comedy thing," you know, not holding anything back.

PHILIP: So you didn't know each other?

RICHARD: We had worked together, but we were definitely three separate camps—actually six, because René brought Marga Gómez, Monica Palacios and the late José Antonio Burciaga together . . .

HERBERT: Odd, odd mixture of different talent and abilities . . .

RIC: I was rapping bilingually and break dancing . . .

HERBERT: And I came on as a reluctant emcee.

RIC: It was a heady mix, at a heady time.

HERBERT: But what happened that night was truly magical. I mean, I think the audience knew, we knew, that this was something really exciting and new and different, you know? There had never been Latino comedy, urban comedy like that before, stand-up comedy.

PHILIP: You were thrown together, but you come from different backgrounds—geographically, culturally. What was going on with this mix?

HERBERT: I was born in San Francisco; my parents are from El Salvador, and I went back to El Salvador to live. And I kind of relearned my culture, you know, I think it was very important to go back because that really gave me an identity. I saw a lot of circus down there, a lot of influential stuff that eventually popped up in my work with Culture Clash. Then I went to California College of Arts and Crafts and got a degree in art, printmaking, silkscreening. I worked at La Raza Graphics

Center for ten years. I was the art director there, so I was doing community, political posters, which I thought was a way of educating and organizing people, and so when I got into theatre, it was just kind of by accident. It was just another tool, another way of expressing or communicating to the people. And I did a lot of community theatre with this group [Teatro Gusto] for six years. But when Culture Clash happened, that was, to me, like I found my place because I was able to be myself, my bicultural self, and it just felt right, very natural and very organic to be in Culture Clash, because we were able to be ourselves . . . the good and the bad.

RIC: I was born in El Salvador. I came up here to the U.S. with my parents not because of the civil war; it was a basic immigrant story. I grew up in San Francisco in the Mission District. I went to San Francisco State University and got sucked into the theatre program there by accident, and joined a theatre group called Teatro Latino. I was from El Salvador but I got very assimilated with the American way of living here, and back then there weren't very many Salvadoreños in the Mission District or in San Francisco, so I gravitated towards the Chicano movement. I graduated in Broadcasting and then I got another degree in Speech Communications. I was doing teatro and it was all kind of angry, political theatre—sometimes a little bit too dogmatic.

When I met Herbert and Richard . . . we all grew up bicultural, in an urban setting. The comedy of Lenny Bruce and Richard Pryor inspired us. We also admired physical comedy like Chaplin and Cantinflas. So we decided to form Comedy Fiesta, which became Culture Clash—the marriage that's still going strong.

RICHARD: I was born in San Diego, California, 1959. We immediately moved to Oakland, California. My dad was teaching at Oakland High School and going to California College of Arts and Crafts. Then we moved further up north—small towns like Marysville, Lincoln. Both parents were educators. But I think the one thing that undeniably influenced me was United Farmworkers Union, the theatre, the art and the literature that the movement spawned. I remember as a young child watching Teatro Campesino—Luis Valdez, Daniel Valdez, Smiley Rojas. And back then they were redefining, or defining, Chicano teatro, on the spot, on the back of pickup trucks. And as a child, I watched that firsthand; and not only that, my dad had a kind of crazy artist collective known as the Royal Chicano Air Force, and they really were the printmakers of the Union.

They were the artists, the artist wing in their Volkswagen buses, and it was a little bit of the hippie thing going on, too. And I got to observe that as a child and soak it up, because not only was the theatre happening onstage, but you might find yourself as a child sitting in Cesar Chavez' office, or Filipino Hall in Delano. I remember as a child, when the first Delano-to-Sacramento farmworker march landed in . . . I believe it was '66 or '67; my mom and a lot of the women would cook for the masses. There were like five to ten thousand farmworkers, camped out in parks. The duties of cooking and all that would fall on the women. And I remember, like three o'clock in the morning, I was helping peel potatoes or something, and everybody was camped out like Zapata's army, except about every five hundredth person, you'd see a light, a flashlight or a lantern, and a kind of slumped-over body that wasn't sleeping, and I asked my mom, "Who are those people?" She goes, "Those are the people who are writing about what's happening right now. Those are the people that are documenting what's going on." That burned an image in my head that one day I wanted to be one of those people.

HERBERT: We all bring in intellectual, cultural, social differences, and that's what makes the group. But underneath it all, we all have the same rage, the same anger. Ric and I have immigrant parents; although Richard is Chicano, there's still that sense that one is an immigrant in this country—there's that rage of being left out, disenfranchised. That unites people, you know, scraggly dogs with problems getting together and becoming this unit, this force.

PHILIP: What was the turning point?

RICHARD: The Public Theater in New York. I think the New York audience . . . I remember them as very brash and loud and vocal, and they liked that in us. We were in your face and—

RIC: We sparred with them. And we started doing some jokes that might have been a little distasteful. Back then, political correctness was huge.

(Chuckles from everybody.)

When we did comedy at La Peña at Berkeley, for instance, you'd get booed or you'd get critiques right there on the spot, and it shaped us. Also at El Teatro Campesino, the elders, we had respect towards them, yet sometimes we didn't give a shit, you know. We would cut down those icons that were protected, from Frida Kahlo to Che Guevara to Julio Iglesias. That's one thing we always did; we always swung swings at the Left as much as the Right.

HERBERT: The writing of *The Mission* was another turning point into "legit" theatre.

PHILIP: Since you were evolving your ideology as a group, your philosophy, your collective way of the doing of the work, were there points where you would have actual sit-down meetings? Or was it a natural evolution?

RICHARD: We have discussed stuff, we've had bitter arguments; we've had almost fistfights about philosophical differences. And sometimes it does come to blows, sometimes physical and mental or spiritual. But I think that we're at this interesting point now, where we're perched on this side of the millennium, and what the fuck's going to happen on the other side? How can we ensure that certain things we've worked and fought for along the way, after fourteen years, can survive. I think, I think Chicanismo as a whole, Central America as a whole, the notion of being an American, all these things are kind of hanging in the balance. We're still very interested in the notion that our people as a whole, men and women, can advance, can do better, and that doesn't mean just projecting positive images. It means exploring dysfunction; it means exploring all those little dark secrets that we've tucked away for so long.

RIC: I also think that the three of us have in a sense morphed, too, to become each other's voice sometimes. I see our work being influenced by each other. Sometimes, I feel I'm saying what Richard would be saying, and sometimes I look at Richard and he's doing a pratfall that normally I would do, and Herbert's doing vice-versa. We've influenced each other from our separate camps, and that's given Culture Clash a strength because not only do we talk about political things, we do silly jokes. We've influenced each other as this triangle, this marriage, and that happens when you're with somebody for fourteen years, there's no way that you cannot influence each other.

RICHARD: Somewhere between *The Mission* and *Bowl of Beings*, and it could have been Ric's shooting, which we talk about in the book, there was a kind of flash point. I think that fearlessness that we had honed, that fearlessness to be irreverent, somehow was applied for our journey into the dark. Culture Clash spent a few years fearlessly exploring the dark, whether it was the way the Mission Indians were treated or it was identity or Ric's shooting, and that's when people started to notice, hey, these Culture Clash guys have a true voice.

PHILIP: How do you create your pieces—nuts and bolts stuff?

RIC: It's like a relay race, you know? You've got the guy who starts, with the baton . . .

HERBERT: It's a germ of an idea . . .

RIC: . . . and he goes out there and jams and talks about it, then gives it to the next guy, and that guy takes it to another level, then that guy gives it to the third, and all of a sudden the three of us are running with this idea . . .

HERBERT: Somebody might add music, which changes the whole feeling.

PHILIP: So you guys work on your feet? Are you jamming inside this room . . .

RICHARD: It's butcher paper! We get on our feet, we start jamming. Herbert comes up with maybe the first draft, and I would take it, then Ric adds something else.

RIC *(With mock indignation)*: I always saw myself as the first draft . . .

HERBERT: Drawings help . . .

PHILIP: Literally or figuratively?

HERBERT: Literally, we visualize . . . I think visually, I'm an artist, so I draw the scene out. . . . I gotta see if it even looks good . . .

RICHARD: And Herbert does every scene, or every idea that we have, in an eight-by-ten . . . and we put it on the rug, floor, wherever we're at . . . we put it—

HERBERT *(Overlapping)*: Just to see if it flows . . .

RICHARD: —down, we see it and then we move it around, and it's really interesting. Because I thought we didn't have a process, but that's been our process now for about eight years.

HERBERT: The script is really not the most important thing, because ultimately, thirty to forty percent changes the minute we show it to the audience. During our workshop process, or during our preview process, that's when the stuff really changes. We really start honing it down. To us, the text is not the ultimate; it's the whole theatrical experience.

PHILIP: Culture Clash has reached the point where you're what Luis Valdez was to you folks when you started out. You are, to a degree, what the younger Chicano/Latino artists would look at as the establishment. Has that been a problem?

RICHARD: Culture Clash has managed, sometimes accidentally and sometimes purposefully, to retain a bit of autonomy, in that we've never really been a part of these institutions that have popped up all over the country, and have really at times created divisions amongst artists and communities. Culture Clash has freely roamed amongst them all and been a part of them and not been a part of them, and as a result, we've been able to stay much more in contact with the young lions that are coming up, and really have their respect. For us, to share the stage with them, whether it be Chusma [Los Angeles-based Chicano comedy group], Nuyorican Rules [New York-based Puerto Rican comedy group], Eighteen Mighty Mountain Warriors [Asian-American comedy group] from the Bay Area, that kind of has a reverberation from the early days when Eric Hayashi [producing manager] at Asian American

Theatre gave us a break. I remember Eric pulling money out of his pocket to give us gas money when there were only three people in the audience. That kind of support you never forget.

PHILIP: You have an expansive, inclusive view of other communities, in other words—the fact that you did things with Asian groups, Puerto Rican groups in New York—it seems you have a strong sense of camaraderie with communities outside of the Chicano/Latino community.

RIC: We've always been outsiders; we've never belonged to one theatre group or one institution. We've always searched for where we could perform better, and not for monetary reasons alone. We get turned on with people that are representing what we want to represent.

HERBERT: We're appealing to youth with our material, and we're still appealing to the old guard, not to mention that we're universal enough that we're appealing to Anglos, blacks, and all that. Now, quite frankly, and we might disagree here, I don't see that happening with the young Chicano/Latino groups. I don't see that kind of openness in their vision and in their worldliness and in their education, where they're going to work with Asian-Americans, where they're going to be more open to other communities.

RICHARD: I think the artist, writer, performer leads the way. We began to lead the way in a sense; we're not just making Latino jokes or Asian jokes or black jokes, and when people come to Little Tokyo and see Culture Clash and an Asian comedy group onstage together it sends out a signal that not only feels right but is essential for our relationships with those artists and also so our work can grow. Artists of color are always gonna feel different in this country than artists of noncolor, and that's OK, it should be celebrated. Again, a kind of fearlessness to exploit and expose and play with those stereotypes and really play with race as a huge issue and the perceptions that Americans might have, I think that's much better than a denial and a stripping of our culture in order to play a Shakespearean character.

HERBERT: Also the reason we do open up to other groups—I think, it's 'cause being together for fourteen years, we've tapped into the Chicano experience—for many years we were hard core.

RIC: Being a group together for fourteen years, we've been able to explore the Chicano experience. We've moved on and explored issues of El Salvador and we've opened it up a little bit more because we've done our homework—we've done certain things and now we're going to do a piece on Aristophanes' *The Birds*. It's going to be the first time that Culture Clash is going to write an adaptation.

RICHARD: It kind of reminds me of this *TIME* magazine article a couple of years ago about the Black Art Renaissance. The point of view of the magazine was that black artists finally transcended racial boundaries. We get that a little bit, too, with people saying, in a sense, you've left the Chicano stuff behind and thank you, you've transcended that and now you're moving on to new, bigger things . . . which I don't entirely agree with. And it bothers me because I know that I'm interested in bringing a Chicano world view to the table. That's a part of my makeup. I will never sever that off. There'll be a Culture Clash point of view. We're not done exploring those issues, and there'll be a new set of issues as we approach the new century.

ACKNOWLEDGMENTS

The following individuals and organizations were instrumental in the growth and success of Culture Clash and the three works in this book.

The founder and godfather René Yañez; founding members Marga Gómez, Monica Palacios and the late José Antonio Burciaga; Reza Abdoh; Actors' Gang Theatre; Rudy Acuña; Steve Adams; Lonnie Alcaraz; Asian American Theater Company, San Francisco; Mauricio Aviles; Carlos Barón; Roberto Bedoya; Nancy Berglass; Berkeley Repertory Theatre; Robert Blacker; Sean San José Blackman; Bill Bushnell; Café Tacuba; The California Arts Council; Juan Carrillo; Casa Zapata at Stanford University; Lalo Cervantes; Cesar's Latin Palace; the late César Chávez; Dan Chumley; Paul Codiga; Sophia Corona; Alex Cox; Tony Curiel; C.X.M.; Gordon Davidson; Nancy de los Santos; Tonantzin Deaztlan; The Doors; Florinda Downer; El Teatro Campesino; Moctesuma Esparza; Phil Esparza; Fountainhead Theatre, Los Angeles; Vicente Franco; David S. Franklin; Fratelli Bologna; Mark Friedman; Galeria de la Raza, San Francisco; Jerry Garcia; Juan Garza; Oscar Garza; Guillermo Gómez-Peña; Gronk; Janine Gross; Guadalupe Cultural Center, San Antonio; Lalo Guerrero; Andrés Gutiérrez; Eric Hayashi; Fran Hernandez;

Mario Hernandez; Juan Felipe Herrera; Danny Hoch; Joan Holden; Bob Howlett; Dolores Huerta; Jorge Huerta, Ph.D.; Lettie Ibarra; INTAR Hispanic American Arts Center, New York; Intersection for the Arts, San Francisco; Japan American Cultural Center, Los Angeles; J.T.; Bob Katz; Tom Kendall; KPFA, Berkeley; KPFK, Los Angeles; Tracy Kramer; La Jolla Playhouse; La Peña Cultural Center, Berkeley; Steve La Ponsie; La Raza Graphics, San Francisco; The Latino Lab; Jordan Levin; The Levinsons; Barrio Logan; José López; The Los Angeles Theatre Center; Linda Lucero; Randall Lum; Luna's Cafe, Sacramento; Mao, Che, Ringo; the late Ralph Maradriaga; Nola Mariano and Circuit Network staff (Sistah Ursula); Cheech Marin; Dena Martínez, France; Des McAnuff; John McCormick; MEChA; John Melfi; Miami Light Project; Mick, Sherri and Trini of Detroit; Mission Cultural Center; El "Gavilán" Molina; José Montoya; Malaquias Montoya; Pete and Norma Navarro; the NEA and the NEA Four; Patricia Nieto; Lane Nishikawa; Al Nodal; Edward James Olmos; Pacifica Radio; Lynn Palmer; Hugo Pedrosa; Mark Pensky; Lisa Peterson; Miguel Piñero; Tony Plana and familia; Lourdes Portillo; Elena Prietto; Dr. Pablo and Anita Prietto; Caren Rabbino; Rage Against the Machine; Geoff Rivas; Roberto Rodríguez; The Royal Chicano Air Force—Sacra; raúl r. "Tapón" salinas; San Diego Repertory Theatre; San Francisco General Hospital; The San Francisco Mime Troupe; Jos Sances; Carlos Santana; Nina Shaw; John Sinclair; Roger Guenveur Smith; South Coast Repertory; the late Barbie Stein; Suicidal Tendencies; Sushi Gallery, San Diego; Richard Talavera; Tamarind Theatre, Los Angeles; The Mark Taper Forum; TENAZ; Toltec Artists; Mark Torrez; The United Farm Workers Union; Luis Valdez; José Luis Valenzuela; Chuy Varela; The Virgen de Guadalupe; Kirk Ward; Diane White; our moms, dads, brothers and sisters and extended familias. Gracias! And the Grandfather Spirit and our fans for believing in us since the "old school daze." Thank you.

GLOSSARY OF TERMS

Abuelo/Abuela: Grandpa/Grandma
Arroz con pollo: chicken and rice
Aztlán: Southwest (the land the Yankees stole)
Bailando: dancing
Balseros: the third wave of exiles from Cuba in the 1990s
Barrio: neighborhood
Cabezón: big head
Cabrón: bastard
Cabrón: Jesse Helms
Cafe Cubano: cheap form of cocaine
Caína: Spanish slang for cocaine
Calcos: shoes
Caló: Chicano slang
Canas: gray hair
Carnal(es): brother(s), friend(s)
Carnitas: fried pork meat
C.C.: Culture Clash, career criminal, Cuban culture, Celia Cruz . . .
Celia Cruz: Queen of Salsa
Chansa: chance
Charo, Rosarita, Maria Conchita Alonso: Latin stereotypes
Che Guevara: Broadway star

Che Guevara: revolutionary figure

Che's Cafe: overpriced Santa Monica restaurant

Chicano: still trying to figure that one out

Chichis: tits

Chingao: Chinese beer

Chingao: fuck

Chingasos: fist blows

Chingón: fucking great

Cholo: homeboy

Chonies: underwear (Jockey, usually)

Chorizo: Mexican sausage

Coconut: a Chicano sellout (brown on the outside, white on the inside)

Cojones: balls (testicles)

Come mierda: shit eater

Communism: outdated Cuban policy

Compañero: comrade

Coño: damn

Corazón: heart

Culo: ass

Dade County Jail: hell

De Colores: Chicano national anthem

Don Colón: Christopher Columbus

El Coocui: boogie man

The Embargo: outdated U.S. policy

Ese: guy

Ganas: willpower

Guajiros: Cuban peasants

Gusano: deragatory term for first-wave exiles from Cuba in the 1960s

Heyoka: sacred clown

Hispanic: government label

H.O.: habitual offender

Huevón: lazy guy

Hurricane Andrew: the Northridge-quake equivalent

Indio: Spanish for "Native American"

Jesse Helms: fried pork meat

La Llorona: boogie woman

La locura cura: craziness cures
La Raza: the people
La Vida: life
Loco: crazy
Macanudo: great
Marielitos: the second wave of exiles from Cuba in the 1980s
MEChA: Chicano student association
The Mission: a predominately Latino district in San Francisco (good taquerias)
The Mission: the artistic mission of three starving Latino comedians
The Mission: an OK movie starring Robert DeNiro
Moco: bugger (snot)
Mocosos: snot-nosed kids
Muerte: death
Mulatto: half black, half Spanish
Nalgas: butt
Nuevo hombre: new man
O.J. (verb): to kill
Órale: all right!
Overtown: area of Miami once called Colored Town or Central Negro District
Pachuco: Mexican-American hipster of the '40s
Pedos: farts
Pelón: bald
Pendejo: fool
Pendejo: Governor Pete Wilson
Piñata: Mexican birthday toy
Pinche: damn
Pinta: jail
Pupusa: Salvadorean quesadilla
Puro pedo: lies
Puta: bitch
Puto: faggot
Ranfla: car
RCAF: Royal Chicano Air Force
Ruca: girlfriend
Salsa: chip dip/festive dance

Santería: Afro-Caribbean religion

Simón: Chicano slang for "yes"

Spanish Town: street term for Little Havana or the Cuban district of Miami

Suerte: luck

Teatro: theatre

Vato: dude

Vendido: sell-out

Yenta: Yiddish for matchmaker

THE MISSION

Photographs by Eric Riel

INTRODUCTION TO *THE MISSION*

by Ricardo Salinas

After years of working together as a comedy troupe, it was time to hunker down and write our first play. It was the summer of 1988, in San Francisco's Mission District, in an old Victorian apartment. The three of us made a pact to lock ourselves in and not come out until we had a finished product. Our elder statesman, the late José Antonio Burciaga, the "Chicano Will Rogers" of the group, had recently quit. He'd been with us since the inception of the group, back when we bore the moniker "Comedy Fiesta," along with comediennes Marga Gómez and Monica Palacios.

Gómez and Palacios had been a duo act long before "Comedy Fiesta," and they left the group to perform on their own in 1986. Shortly after their departure, our godfather, Rene Yañez, who first conceived of the group, came up with the new name for the remaining four "musketeros": Culture Clash, the first Chicano/ Latino comedy troupe in the whole pinche world! The name was partly inspired by the success of the British invasion of the '80s, particularly the band Culture Club. But the name also signified the culture clash of Latinos against mainstream America, as well as the culture clash between the different Latino races.

For the next two years, we played up and down California, all across the country, in festivals, benefits, teatros, conventions, colleges, the Joseph Papp Public Theater in New York, street fairs. Our new name was getting out there. But José had grown tired of doing one-night stands and the touring circuit in the company of three rambunctious vatos who were in their mid-twenties. Since he had two children who were entering middle school and high school, he decided to focus on his family life as well as his writing and art projects. In the spring of '88, he bid us adios. The departure was amicable, aside from a few regañadas and a contract for a hundred bucks that stated we could use any of his material if we asked permission and remembered to credit him, tan tan. He went back to Casa Zapata, the Chicano dormitory at Stanford where he lived with his wife Cecilia and two children, Rebeca and Toño.

So there we were, regrouped, los tres payasos, Richard Montoya, Ricardo Salinas and Herbert Siguenza, a.k.a. Culture Clash, embarking on a mission, in the Mission, to write our first play, *The Mission*.

Prior to *The Mission*, a typical Culture Clash show was cabaret-style without a narrative. We each took our "star" turn with material that we had written on our own. We collaborated on sketches and punched up each other's jokes. There was no director, lighting designer, sound designer, costume designer, dramaturg or publicist. We did it all—a true collective.

Despite the cultural, social and political implications of our subject matter, the emphasis was always on the funny, the satirical, what would invoke the biggest laugh, which pratfall would work best. Our foremost objective was to be entertainers. And following close behind, we were social commentators. It was "informed slapstick," as one reviewer put it. And most important, we explored the simple fact that we were born or grew up here in the United States with English as our dominant language, and that's how we delivered our punchlines, with some Spanglish for sabor and hardly any Spanish. With comedy, we could address socially relevant issues but disguise them with wit. Now it was time to put all these ingredients together into a cohesive storyline with a beginning, middle and end.

How would we approach writing a play that would encompass the many styles that we'd developed through the years? In the late '80s, the stand-up comedy clubs were in full swing, especially in the San Francisco Bay Area. These venues were never for us, abounding with too many racist and sexist jokes, and we purposely stayed away. Our political correctness would not allow us to perform there. Besides, we have always considered ourselves a "theatre group."

Our take on humor is influenced by the comedy of North American film and television personalities like Martin and Lewis, Jackie Gleason, Lucille Ball and Ernie Kovacs, and stand-up comedians such as Lenny Bruce, Richard Pryor, Freddy Prinze, Whoopi Goldberg, Paul Rodriguez. True media babies, Culture Clash was weaned on pop staples, MTV and the situation comedies of the 1960s and 1970s—"Dy-no-mite!" The Martin Scorsese film *The King of Comedy* and Mel Brooks' *The Producers* inspired our writing.

The Mission is a synthesis of many traditions. It is a play about us: Richard, Ric and Herbert, a culmination of three separate lives coming together in a desperate plea to tell the world about our dilemma. It is a semi-autobiographical romp about three frustrated Latino actors from San Francisco's Mission District trying to break into show biz. It opens in 1776 at Mission Dolores, where the sadomasochistic Spanish Father Junipero Serra tries to save his little neophytes with true "Western" culture. The action leaps, via a peyote vision quest, to the present, where we meet three out-of-work actors. After performing in racist nightclubs, auditioning in degrading casting calls, being turned down for acting either too Hispanic or not Hispanic enough, the trio decides to kidnap Julio Iglesias (the great-great-great-great-great-great-grandson of Junipero Serra) for a shot at national fame.

Reflecting on those days when we imprisoned ourselves in that old Victorian, we really did set out on a mission that has continued throughout our years together—to spread the message of protest on behalf of all disenfranchised Latino actors trying to make it in the entertainment business. Though it was written ten years ago, the message is just as relevant today, unfortunately. In 1997, according to a study by the National Council of La Raza, a Washington-based Latino advocacy group, Latinos account for only 1 percent of television characters and 2.5 percent of film characters.

As Latino actors, we knew that we had to write our own roles, our own stories. There are millions of Latinos, like us, who are bilingual, bicultural and proud of both their American and Latino roots, who are not being represented. Except for the once-every-three-years "Latin-themed production," we weren't being asked to audition for the major theatre venues. When we wrote *The Mission*, it wasn't a showcase for Hollywood. It was to prove to ourselves that we weren't merely stand-up comedians, sketch players or improv artists. We wanted to legitimize ourselves in the theatre community as actors and playwrights, to stake our claim. The theatre critics hadn't seen our previous endeavors because of the cabaret-style setting. With a full-length play and well-rounded characters, our material was out there to be judged.

The world premiere of *The Mission* was on October 5, 1988 at Intersection for the Arts in San Francisco. Founded in the mid-sixties, the Intersection was a prestigious not-for-profit institution with a great track record for putting on well-known performers and theatre acts. In the summer of 1988, we received a phone call from Paul Codiga, who was the Theatre Director of the Inter-section at the time. He had seen us perform one of our comedy shows and wanted to book us for the fall. Along with the literary director, Roberto Bedoya, he wondered if we had a play we could present. Of course we said yes—and that's when we started work on *The Mission*.

After we made that commitment to the Intersection, Richard Montoya moved from Sacramento to the Mission District, where Herbert and I both grew up. His relocation proved to be a turn-ing point in our careers and partnership as a theatre troupe. The three of us put our day jobs on hold. Like an old Mickey Rooney and Judy Garland movie, we got excited, and gathered up all our resources and talents to mount a show! We began writing what we knew best: our story, of course with some added satire.

While we were writing *The Mission*, there was a campaign to make Father Junipero Serra a saint. Some thought the Pope should canonize him for being the founder of the California missions and converting the Indians to Christianity. We thought otherwise. According to some documentation, Father Junipero Serra was no saint. He was a perfect target for us to lampoon. Incidentally, he still hasn't reached sainthood.

The entire production budget for *The Mission* was three hundred and nineteen dollars. With the help of our friends, family, volunteers, peers (Richard Talavera, Lalo Cervantes, and Rene Yañez), plus the friendly spirits of the Intersection (it was formerly a funeral home), the play was a success!

The Mission toured around the state and across the country. When it played at El Teatro Campesino in San Juan Bautista, it was the first time we used a director, Tony Curiel. Tony helped develop additional narrative and comedy bits. And then *The Mission* premiered at the Los Angeles Theatre Center's black box theatre in August 1990 directed by José Luis Valenzuela. It did so well that it moved to a three-hundred-seat theatre in that complex, with a bigger budget, better technical support and a set designed by Los Angeles artist Gronk. We dedicated the play to legendary Chicano singer and songwriter Lalo Guerrero. Paradoxically, we had written a play that indicted the Hollywood industry, but it was those same people who filled the theatre night after night. Mission accomplished!

PRODUCTION HISTORY

The Mission received its premiere in October 1988 at Intersection for the Arts in San Francisco, California.

In August 1990, *The Mission* was produced at the Los Angeles Theatre Center with the following cast and creative contributors:

Ensemble	Richard Montoya, Ric Salinas and Herbert Siguenza
Director	José Luis Valenzuela
Sets	Gronk
Costumes	Herbert Siguenza
Lights	José López
Sound	Richard Montoya and Ric Salinas
Video	Richard Montoya, Ric Salinas, Herbert Siguenza
Stage Managers	David S. Franklin and John Paul Melfi

In September 1993, *The Mission* was produced at La Jolla Play-house with the following cast and creative contributors:

Ensemble	Richard Montoya, Ric Salinas and Herbert Siguenza
Director	Tony Curiel
Sets	Victoria Petrovich
Costumes	Herbert Siguenza
Lights	José López
Sound	Richard Montoya and Ric Salinas
Video	Richard Montoya, Ric Salinas and Herbert Siguenza with Mark Friedman
Stage Manager	Tina Shackleford

The Mission also had runs at the Asian American Theatre Company, San Francisco, California; El Teatro Campesino, San Juan Bautista, California; and the Attic Theatre, Detroit, Michigan.

LIST OF SCENES

Act One
Serra Overture, *1776*
Peyote Dreams
Time Travel Sequence
Mission Apartment, *1990s*
Tommy P's Comedy Club, *that evening*
Taqueria Serra, *the next morning*
The Auditions, *that day*
Mission Apartment, *that evening*

Act Two
The California Camino Real Tour Audition, *two weeks later*
Spic Talk, *that evening*
Mission Apartment, *that evening*
California Camino Real Tour, *next evening*
Epilogue

Note
The beginning of the play is set in eighteenth-century San Francisco, California. The upstage center area is used as the Mission court-yard. The downstage center area is flanked by a very contemporary apartment which must not be exposed for the opening "Serra Overture" scene.

ACT ONE

SCENE ONE
Serra Overture, 1776

Darkness.

Four Mission bells toll and a Native American funeral chant is heard. Moments later two Indios enter carrying candles. They cross center stage and salute the Four Directions, then turn upstage toward the altar/pedestal.

The Indios bend down and each light a candle on the floor; then, they each light a candle on the second step of the pedestal. They are precise in observing their ritual. Following the lighting of the candles, the Indios kneel, each holding a candle at eye-level. They blow the candles out.

The funeral chant music segues into European religious music. As this music builds, the lights slowly expose Father Serra on his pedestal— first his feet, then his legs, then his face, and then his hands outstretched to the heavens.

Father Serra descends a step at a time assisted by the Indios, who remain on their knees until Father Serra passes before them. The Indios rise, turn toward the audience, follow Father Serra a step downstage, and kneel again to receive communion.

An overly dramatic narration is heard:

VOICEOVER: October 9th, 1776. The sixth mission under the direction of Father Junipero Serra was completed in California. San Francisco de Assisi was the crown jewel of all the missions in the Brave New World.

One man, one vision, one million Indios wiped out by murder, disease and torture. And, at least five known cases of the dreaded jock itch.

(One of the Indios scratches his crotch area. Father Serra grabs the Indios by their ears.)

Father Serra loved his little savages. No Indian was buried before his time. And, by the grace of God, he set out to make these naked creatures "Men of Reason." The beloved Mission Dolores was built next to the "Stream of Sorrows," known today as the "San Francisco Bathhouse of Sorrows." Thousands of tourists lose their collective chonies there each year in the barrio streets of their mind, de chamberline, hear my rhyme, tecate with lime, commit a crime, do the time, OK, that's enough. Ladies and gentlemen, the anatomy of a Culture Clash—The Mission!

(Music swells, underscoring Father Serra's following monologue.)

FATHER SERRA: Oh, my little brown ones. What mischief have we been in today? My little savages, digo, my little sheep. When I found these little creatures they were living in the cracks of the earth. Now, they say no to crack! Verdad!

(With that, Father Serra yanks the Indios' heads back by their hair.)

I took away their pagan dances and gave them true culture! La opera, el ballet, los Gypsy Kings! I took away their primitive tongue and taught them Español, and you better speak Spanish now, my little ones, before English becomes the official language! I took away their religion; now they fear God! And, with a little help from the whip, the gun and the cross . . . *(He pulls a large blade from a cross)* they respect me, despite my lisp.

One day the world will recognize me. In fact, I was almost canonized by the Pope himself. Yes, I'm feeling a little smug about the whole affair, and why not? The guilt I have instilled in these Indios is the very same guilt passed on to future generations of Indios, Mestizos, and struggling Latino actors. I founded twenty-one California missions. My favorite is Mission Dolores in San Francisco of a sissy, digo Assisi. I envision a city here with great bridges, of pyramids, of Forty-Niners and of Giants. One day they will name hospitals and schools after me. One day they will construct a stupid statue of me on Highway 280! Yet, there are people who question whether I have performed any miracles. My friends, let me show you un milagro.

(Father Serra slaps his hand in a command. Indio #1 instinctively rolls forward like a trained dog.)

Parate! Bestia!

(Indio #1 stands.)

Sing, my little neophyte. Sing, my little California raisin!

INDIO #1: Fa la la la la la . . . *(Turns to Father Serra for approval)*

FATHER SERRA: You were flat like a tortilla. Donde esta mi whip? Sing again . . . sing . . . sing!

(Father Serra begins to flog the Indio with a leather whip.)

Sing, sing, sing! *(He is in a flogging sadomasochistic frenzy)* Stop! Stop! Vale, vale, you have reached your flogging quota for the day. Go!

(Indio #1 turns back upstage to join Indio #2. As he turns, he exposes to the audience a perfect Tic-Tac-Toe game on his back from the bloody flogging.)

FATHER SERRA: Oh, I don't know what to do with these Indios. I give them books, college, and I still get ring around the collar. Oh well, I guess I'll go to the Friars Club and have a smoke. Why do I speak like Count Chocula? *(Walks upstage to the Indios. To Indio #2:)* And, I better not catch you spray-painting graffiti on the mission walls! *(Turns to Indio #1)* And as for you, do not worry about your back. A little lime juice will help.

(With that, Father Serra whips Indio #1 on the back again. Indio #1 contorts in pain. Father Serra crosses himself.)

And God bless you, son. And remember, *(Chanting)* Dominus Pizza delivers!

(Father Serra exits. Indio #2 helps Indio #1 from the ground; they struggle. Indio #1 is singing, half-dazed from the whipping. Indio #2 slaps some sense into him.

Indio #1 speaks to Indio #2 in exaggerated sign language. Indio #2 responds with faster sign language.)

INDIO #1: Wait, wait, my brother; you always go too fast.

(Indio #2 slows down.
Then, the Indios stop signing and start speaking in mock English accents.)

Yes, what you say is true, my hardened-nippled brother. Father Serra is . . . an asshole!

INDIO #2: Why do you refuse to speak in our own language? You are assimilating, and why must you pretend to be a singer? You have told me on numerous occasions that you want to be a stand-up comedian.

INDIO #1: What you say is true, but the friars do not allow me to tell jokes in our native tongue. Why just last night at the Monks' Lounge, I told a joke in our language and I received fifty lashes! Would you like to see the joke? *(He gestures the joke in native sign language)* Do you like it?

INDIO #2: Yes, but I saw that on Indio Star Search last night.

INDIO #1: I remember a time not long ago when we didn't have to hold in our tummies so hard. A time when our people were proud and unafraid.

INDIO #2: We used to pray to the Grandfather Spirit and we respected Mother Earth.

INDIO #1: And then the Spaniards moved in, high atop their horses, and they tried to fix up everybody's hut and put our children in Montessori schools. And, there went the barrio!

INDIO #2: And now our days are filled with hard labor, endless hours of work, pesticides. And we have no medical or dental benefits. Oh, why couldn't César Chávez have been born now?

INDIO #1: Hark! My foolish Jerry Garcia-looking brother, these Spaniards do not understand nonviolent protest. They will kill us for sure! What we need to do is mount an attack, a revolution! We must educate the others *(Secretive)* I know a printer in Berkeley who can print us 10,000 flyers for a bushel of corn and a pair of Birkenstocks! What is it, my Three-Dog-Night-looking brother? Why does it appear that you are smelling freshly laid buffalo manure?

INDIO #2: Oh, my large-buttocked friend, the flogging has gone to your head like bad peyote.

(Indio #2 slaps Indio #1 on his flogged back.)

INDIO #1: Ouch!

INDIO #2: Sorry. What I am trying to say is that our brothers from the south tried an insurrection and it failed. This is our destiny. History is not on our side. *(Singing)* Que será, será. Whatever will be, will be.

INDIO #1: The future's not ours to see . . .

INDIO #2: Que Serra, Serra . . .

INDIO #1: There you go again with that Doris Day existential buffalo crap again. I have no time for your Kafka novel. You are falling for the Spanish Manifesto. I will mount a revolution, myself. Because, my Credence Clearwater Revival Brother, at the end of this tunnel of death, I see a light!

INDIO #2: Light, my brother?

INDIO #1: Bud Lite! *(Pulls out beer can from a sack)* No! There.

INDIO #2: The exit sign?

INDIO #1: No, higher.

INDIO #2: Hi-yer?

INDIO #1: Hi-yah.

INDIO #2: Hi-yah?

(They perform a mock Native American chant and dance.)

INDIO #1: AND #2: Hi-yah, hi-yah, hi-yah, hi-yah.

INDIO #1: Stop that! See, high above the ridge. A thousand points of light, a burning bush and a dead quail. Surely it is a sign. I must warn the others, I must go. *(He exits)*

INDIO #2: My brother, my brother . . . my heart bleeds for him. Too many floggings, too much MTV. I must transcend this reality. I must call upon the Grandfather Spirit and make contact with future generations and warn them of the evil and slaughter to come.

Peyote Dreams

A fusion of drums and synthesized music fades in rapidly. Indio #2 sits back at the altar. He reaches into his bag and pulls out a pipe. He tries to light the pipe with a twig, tosses the twig and lights up with a child-proof Bic lighter.

Music changes to rap beat. Indio #2 rises and performs a Native American dance that transforms into modern hip-hop movements. He starts to rap:

INDIO #2: Ruler of the moon, ruler of the sun
 The planted seed has just begun
 A fire power luminating up the skies
 Beware of the truths made from the lies

 In the echo chamber of your soul and mind
 Don't be misled by these changing times
 I see steamy streets in an urban land
 Corner after corner where the rats command
 Chicano warriors in barrio warfare
 Sacrifice executed through a dare
 Relics of bygone yesteryear

 Emerge into the future and all seem to fear
 Day by day we are cast away
 And the sleeping giant has nothing to say
 Acculturation process it's never explained
 We got no leaders it's time to complain
 But our minds are blown
 We fight among our own
 On our tender young fire from the rain
 Education not worth the pain
 The shame, the lies, the alibis
 The hip, the jive, the quick streetwise
 The chase is on to catch your breath

You gasp for air only to find death
The wretched stench of existing life
The pointless edge of the killer's knife

I'm living now that far-off reality
My brothers tortured, mistreated excessively
Flogging to instill discipline
And I don't even know what was our sin
40,000 Indians lie in unmarked graves
No one owned the land but now we're slaves?

The smell of incense travels through the air
Peyote dreams that take me there
An nochipa tlaticpac
Zan achica ye nican
An nochipa tlalticpac
Zan achica ye nican
No siempre para en la tierra: solo un poco aquí
No siempre para en la tierra: solo un poco aquí

Oh Grandfather Spirit
Take me to the many moons of tomorrow
Show me the path, show me the light
Show me the truth Grandfather Spirit!

SCENE THREE

Time Travel Sequence

Lights and set change rapidly around Indio #2 as he travels through time to the Mission District, early '90s. He watches as the world around him transforms. He walks to a TV monitor; his energy turns the TV on; he peers in wonderment. He grabs a ghetto blaster and shakes it; it blasts out at him. Startled, he throws it on the couch; he hears someone coming and, frightened, jumps behind a couch.

Mission Apartment, 1990s

Richard, a tall, dark and handsome young Latino, enters. He has long hair, wears a leather jacket and torn-up jeans. He swaggers in from his bedroom through the kitchen door, slaps on the kitchen light and wildly dances around the apartment to the Guns N' Roses tune "Welcome to the Jungle." He grabs an acoustic guitar and starts playing rock-star.

Herbert, an older, dark, handsome Latino, enters. He comes in from the outside through the living room door. He is dressed like Michael Jackson. He is downcast and grouchy. There is confetti strewn on his jacket. Richard does not notice him. Herbert walks to the TV and ghetto blaster and shuts them off.

RICHARD: Hey! What the. . . . I'm getting psyched up to . . .

HERBERT: I had a bad day, OK?

RICHARD: What the. . . . You had a kiddie show today. How did it go?

HERBERT: I bombed, Richard. I bombed at the kids' party. The mocosos were hitting me instead of the piñata!

RICHARD: Get a hold of yourself, Herb. Haven't I been telling you the kiddie circuit is a killer? *(Pulls dart out of Herbert's head)* These kids don't give a shit about you! C'mon, chalk it up as a bad day. Some of us have bad days . . . *(Gloating)* some of us have good days.

HERBERT: What are you so happy about?

RICHARD: What's today?

HERBERT: I don't know.

RICHARD: C'mon, think!

HERBERT: It's rent day, we're behind in the rent!

RICHARD: No, dude. Look at the *(Anglo accent)* Quetzalcoatl Aztec calendar. Today is the day I open up at Tommy P's, the number one comedy club in the whole pinche Bay Area!

HERBERT: Tommy P's, huh? So what can I say, I'm happy for you, Rich. On the other hand, everything is caving in on me, even my love life.

RICHARD: What happened?

HERBERT: I caught my girlfriend cheating.

RICHARD: My god, with who?

HERBERT: With the entire horn section of the Miami Sound Machine.

RICHARD: Herb, as your homeboy, your roommate and carnal, I am truly sorry. Can I use that for my comedy show?

HERBERT: No, you can't use that in your comedy show! It's my life, man! You make everything into a goddamned joke! Look at me! I look ridiculous! My career is going down the tubes. I'm not bad, I'm sad!

RICHARD: Yes, look at yourself, Herbert! What have I been telling you for the last five years? You're wasting your time in this Viva la Raza, Chicano teatro crap.

HERBERT: It's important to me.

RICHARD: OK, fine, it's important. But, you can't stay in the barrio all your life, you need to go mainstream. *La Bamba*, dude!

HERBERT: I know that, Richard, but I'm not going to compromise my integrity, my material, to satisfy some white audience. I'm not going to do caca peepee jokes all my life. Is that what you're going to do tonight . . . caca peepee jokes?

RICHARD (*Sarcastic*): No, Herbert, tonight I thought I would do some really whimsical Frida Kahlo and Dostoyevsky material 'cause I think that will go over well with suburban housewives! I'm going to do what I need to do, that's my whole point!

HERBERT: Great, you go ahead and do that homophobic, sexist shit. They'll love that.

RICHARD: When did you join a sensitive male collective? You know what your problem is?

HERBERT: What?

RICHARD: You don't try hard enough.

HERBERT: I don't try hard enough? Let me tell you something. I've been doing theatre in this town for ten years. The repertory companies never call us to do Shepard, O'Neill, Beckett or Shakespeare! No, they just call us for that once-a-year Latino play they're producing on their second stage. And, you know why they're doing it? For the funding! Yeah, that's what all the foundations want to hear. So, we all compete for these crumbs and one of us gets the part. Once the play is over, they don't call us back; they just say thank you and adios, motherfucker!

RICHARD: You are so negative, man. You are not getting called for Shepard, Beckett or Shakespeare not because of the color of your skin, pal, it's because of your attitude. I can see it now; you walk in with this tortilla chip on your shoulder: *(Mocking)* "I'm a Chicano actor, I'm a struggling actor." It doesn't work that way, man. *(Pause)* Let me ask you a question, Herb. You were born and raised right here in the barrio, the Mission, right?

HERBERT *(Proudly)* : Simón.

RICHARD: See, I can tell. I was raised with white people . . .

HERBERT *(Pause)*: I can tell.

RICHARD: My point is this, smart-ass: you have to be able to walk into any situation, nightclub, theatre, whatever it is, look your audience right in the eye, and no matter if they are black, brown, white, you give them everything you got, get your check, and get out. That's my philosophy, and that's why I'm getting gigs at Tommy P's, and you are being mistaken for piñatas at kiddie shows!

HERBERT *(Defeated)*: You're right, Rich, and I'm glad you can do it. Obviously, I can't.

RICHARD: Yes, you can!

(The following is in dramatic soap-opera style.)

HERBERT: Richard, I have something terrible to tell you.

RICHARD: My god, what is it, Herb?

HERBERT: I got a nine-to-five job today!

RICHARD: No! Herbert, you didn't!

HERBERT *(Sobbing)*: I start tomorrow.

RICHARD: Turn around, look me in my blue eye, and say it isn't so!

HERBERT: I dreaded this day, Rich. I never wanted a day job.

RICHARD: Culture Clash says good-bye to a hell of a good actor and great friend. You know what this means, Herbert?

HERBERT: No, what?

RICHARD: More work for me and Ric.

HERBERT: You asshole. Hey, Rich, you won't believe the uniform I have to wear at work. I got it in my room, let me show you.

RICHARD: You have to wear a uniform at work? Working at a bank?

HERBERT: No, no, I'll be right back.

(Herbert begins to exit but is stopped by Richard.)

RICHARD: Herb . . .

HERBERT: What?

RICHARD: You know I never said this before, but out of the three of us in Culture Clash, I always knew . . .

HERBERT: Yeah?

RICHARD: I would be the first one to make it.

HERBERT: That's because you're a *sellout. (He exits)*

RICHARD: Sellout, huh! I been a Chicano longer than you . . . *(To himself)* Don't let him get you down, you got a gig, c'mon, psyche up. OK. Tommy P's, there's an audience, here goes my first joke. *(Holding up picture cards to audience)*

This is your brains.
This is your brains on drugs.
This is your brains on drugs with chorizo.
Chorizo is a terrible thing to waste.
No! *(Worried)* It'll never work.

(Richard sits at a coffee table in front of the couch. He thumbs through a history book on the table and reads out loud about Father Serra and the Costanoan Indios. Ric/Indio #2 peeks cautiously over the couch.

Ric, coming out of (or off of) his peyote dream/trip, studies Richard. Dazed and confused, Ric sneaks behind Richard, crouches next to Richard's ear and screams a bird/hawk call. This startles Richard, who reacts by pushing Ric onto the couch. Both are startled.)

RICHARD: What the hell are you doing, Salinas?

RIC: Shut up.

RICHARD: Man, why are you dressed like that?

RIC: SHUT UP!!!!!

RICHARD: Ric?
RIC: Ric? *(Pointing to Richard)*
RICHARD: Rich.
RIC *(To himself)*: Rich.

(Frustrated with the confusion, Richard slaps Ric, who returns the slap. More slaps, until Richard pushes Ric away.)

RICHARD: Tell me what's going on! How come your nipples are hard?
RIC: Oh, man, I was doing this performance piece at a really cool art gallery. I was trying something new for their Chicano Night series. It was an Aztec Rap. Man, you should have seen me, Rich. Rapping, Imix, ik, akbal, mulOOOOOOKK!

(Ric is freaking out. Richard covers Ric's mouth to try to calm him down.)

RICHARD: Ric! I want you to calm down, your pal is right here. Just wipe the booger off your mustache and tell me what the hell happened to you.
RIC: I was about to go on, and someone slipped me some peyote in my nachos. I was in the middle of my rap when I felt something weird inside of me, like a spirit going through me. That's when I saw this Indio, and he took me by the hand, and we began to fly. We flew back in time, here to the Mission, but it was a long time ago. And, I was an Indio, with a lot of other Indios. And, we were working, working hard, in fact too hard. That's when I saw Father Serra and he began hitting us and making us work even harder. I mean he began taking away our customs, our religion, our language, he was all over us, hitting us, whipping, flogging, and we were fighting and women . . . estaban desnudas con sus chichis y el cabrón de Serra nos pegaba bien gacho . . .
RICHARD: Ric, hold on, buddy. You know you really scare me when you speak Mexican. Now, stop talking about Father Serra that way. He was a good man; they're going to make him a saint, for Christ's sake.

RIC *(Pause)*: He was a fucker.

RICHARD: Oh, you better be careful, that's bad karma.

RIC: Things haven't changed, Richard. Things haven't changed. I'm going to work on my altar, 'cause we need good karma.

(Ric goes to a corner of the room where he keeps an altar on a Radio Flyer. Herbert enters from the kitchen, wearing a friar's robe—his uniform for his new job at Taqueria Serra: Heavenly Tacos. Ric does not see him come in. Herbert crosses straight over to Richard on the couch.)

HERBERT: Hey, Richard, you like it? Pretty cool, huh? This is my new work uniform.

RICHARD: That's killer, dude . . . not bad.

(Ric wheels his altar over and notices Herbert in his Father Serra outfit. Ric charges at Herbert.)

RIC: INDIAN KILLER, INDIAN KILLER!

(Ric leaps onto a chair, dives off and tackles Herbert. They spin and drop to the floor. Richard pulls them apart. Herbert is stunned.)

HERBERT: What the fuck is wrong with you?

RICHARD: Are you OK, Herbert?

RIC: Herbert?

RICHARD: That's Herbert, asshole.

(Ric runs back to his altar, takes holy water and sprinkles Herbert and his robe.)

RIC: Take it off! Take it off!

HERBERT: No! Hey, stop that! I paid forty dollars for this. It's my uniform for my job at the taqueria tomorrow. *(Notices Ric dressed as Indio)* Hey, why are you dressed like that? You look like Kunta Kinte. Hey, he's got whip marks on his back! *(Pause)* Still going out with that freaky chick, huh?

RIC: Oh, man, that was some strong peyote.

HERBERT: PEYOTE? You know the Culture Clash rules: *no drugs* . . . except on Tuesdays.

RICHARD: Hey, Mother Superior, why don't you just mellow out? Somebody slipped him something. He's had a hard night. You really have to wear that thing to make tacos?

HERBERT: That's right.

RICHARD: What a fucking joke.

HERBERT *(Angry)*: Joke? No, you want to see a joke? Here's a joke, Richard. *(Grabs a piece of paper)* Eviction notice, pal. An eviction notice from Mr. Chow. We don't pay rent around here. We don't pay bills. We don't pay for food . . .

RIC: I got the munchies bad.

HERBERT: Shut up! This is pitiful. You know, in this whole household, I'm the only one who wears the pants around here.

RICHARD: You have on a dress, Herb.

RIC: Has anybody seen my pants?

HERBERT: Oh, this is splendid. I got a performance artist, peyote-smoking, frequent-flying Juan Diego drug addict over there. And over here I have a prima donna.

RICHARD: I'm a prima donna?

HERBERT: Yes! And, you're spoiled.

RICHARD: I'm spoiled? *(Covers his ears with his hands)* Am not, am not, am not.

HERBERT: Oh, look at you. . . . You're not going to starve. I don't have a mom like you who's going to bring me tortillas, arroz, frijolitos. No weekly rations for me. You know what I ate when I grew up?

RICHARD: What?

HERBERT: Wonder Bread. And, it was only toasted on one side, because our toaster was broken. I had a stiff brown side and a mushy white side. And, I would eat this toast with my TV dinner while watching *I Dream of Jeannie* on a black-and-white TV set.

RICHARD: Let me try to get some perspective on this little pathetic story, Herbert. You are going to make some tacos in that ridiculous-looking outfit because you had a fucked-up childhood? UUGGH! Excuse me. That's great, Herb, you go on with your bad self and make your tacos. I'm going to make people laugh. Is that OK with you? And, you know, thanks for reminding me. I'm going to do some stereotypes tonight. *(To Ric)* Is that OK with you, Carlos Castañeda? 'Cause that's what they want to see at Tommy P's. *(Like Speedy Gonzalez)* Arriba! Arriba! *(Does Chinese, slanting his eyes, then grabs his crotch and acts "black")* Is that OK, Uncle Fester? 'Cause you fuckin' with the kid now, don't you ever fuck with the kid, you just sit there and kick it with crack head. You taco-making, motherfucking fool.

(Richard exits through the living room door. Herbert puts his head down on the kitchen table, upset. Ric stares at Herbert from the altar, then crosses to him.)

RIC: Pink hearts, yellow moons, orange stars, green clovers, Lucky Charms, they're magically delicious. I'm cuckoo for Cocoa Puffs, cuckoo for Cocoa Puffs. . . . I'm cuckoo for Cocoa Puffs, cuckoo for Cocoa Puffs!

(Ric maniacally chases Herbert around the apartment.)

HERBERT *(Scared)*: You stay away from me!

(They run offstage. Blackout.)

SCENE FIVE

Tommy P's Comedy Club

VOICEOVER: Thank you, everybody. Welcome out to "Tommy P's" here in the beautiful suburbs of San Francisco. Tonight we have a young comedian from the Mission District. That's where most of you get your cars ripped off from. Ha ha ha. Maybe when he's done, he'll make us all a burrito or something. Ha ha. Oh, c'mon now. Keep it down. No more penis jokes. Let's give a big "Tommy P" round of applause for Richard Montoya. Ricky Ricardo. C'mon!

(Audience applause is heard. Richard faces upstage, his back to the audience. A spotlight hits him. He is seen in silhouette. Richard struggles with his comedic material; the audience grows restless, starts to heckle and shout racial epithets. The booing and the restaurant ambiance cross-fade to Jerry Garcia's "Mission in the Rain." Richard, dejected, bows and exits. Lights and music fade.)

Taqueria Serra

Lights and upbeat Mexican music come up. José #1 and José #2 dance and gossip and prepare for a busy day at Taqueria Serra: Heavenly Tacos. Music fades out. Herbert enters. José #1 and #2 speak with heavy Mexican accents.

JOSÉ #1: Hola, can I help you?

HERBERT: Hola, I'm Herbert.

JOSÉ #1: Nice to meet you.

HERBERT: I came to work today.

JOSÉ #1: Oh, very nice. *(Pause)* Where do you work?

HERBERT *(Confused)*: No, you don't understand. I came to work here, for you. You called me, remember? I'm Herbert.

JOSÉ #1: Herbert—oh! Oh, si, si, si. Oye, José, el nuevo muchacho que va trabajar con nosotros. I call him yesterday. Good. We begin work now. Walk this way.

(Herbert imitates the way José #1 walks.)

Oh, I'm very sorry. My name is José 1, and this is my cousin, José 2

HERBERT *(To José #2)*: Nice to meet you, José.

JOSÉ #1 *(Correcting)*: No, José 2.

HERBERT: My cousin's name is José, too.

JOSÉ #1: José 2?

HERBERT: No, just José.

JOSÉ #1: That's my name, too.

HERBERT: José 2?

JOSÉ #2: No, that's my name, you damned . . .

HERBERT: Oh, I get it. José 1 and José 2. I'm Herbert.

JOSÉ #1: I thought it was Herberto.

HERBERT: It's Herbert, too.

JOSÉ #2 *(Angry)*: Is your name Herbert, Herberto, or Herbert 2?

HERBERT *(Defeated)*: Just call me Angélica.

JOSÉ #1: Very well. We have to train you very, very fast. You see, because looky, the gringos are already lining up around the corner.

HERBERT: I never understood that. There are ten taquerías on this block, and all the gringos decide to line up for this one. Why is that?

JOSÉ #1: The gringos don't know any better. They see one gringo lining up, and they say, *(Like gringo)* "Oh, honey, this place must be good. Let's give it a try." That's when they come in and order the tacos al cabrón. OK, we must train you now. Vamos

pues. Let's begin. *(Rapidly)* First you take the order, give it to me, I steam the tortilla, I pass it down to José 2 and he chop, chop, chop and give back to me. I make taco, give it to you, and you call out the number. OK? Bueno, you try.

HERBERT *(Very politely)*: Number 86, is there a number 86 in the house?

JOSÉ #1: Me lleva la chingada. . . . Idiota! You are doing it all wrong. The gringos don't want to hear that. The gringos want to hear authentic beaner accent. Mira, José 2, enséñale. Show him.

JOSÉ #2 *(Super loud)*: NUMBER 54!! Cincuenta-y-cuatro!!!!

HERBERT: OK, I got it. Number 54!!! Cincuenta-y-cuatro!!

JOSÉ #1 AND JOSÉ #2: Very good.

JOSÉ #2: Bueno, open the door . . . cuidado con los gringos.

(José #1 mimes opening the door and a crowd pushing by him.)

JOSÉ #1: One at a time, one at a time!

(The three workers begin to mime taco-making activities in a frenzied conveyer-belt pace.)

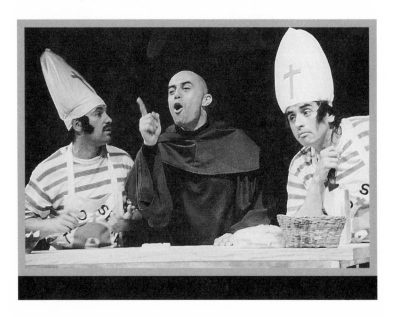

HERBERT: A pork burrito, sure. José 1, vegetarian burrito. Number 26! Número 26. Twenty! What? Polo? No, that's "pollo." Lengua? That's tongue. Sesos? That's brains. Menudo? That's stomach lining. Burrito? That's a little Mexican donkey about this big. 27! 28! What? A quesadilla with no cheese? Get out of here!

(The work pace accelerates.)

Number 29! Número veinte nueve! Burrito! Number 30! Número treinta! Taco! Number 31! Número treinta y uno! Number 32! 33! 34! 35! 36! 37! Estop! Estop! Estop! I mean, STOP! STOP! I can't take this anymore! *(He takes off his friar gown)*

JOSÉ #2: Porque? Why?

HERBERT *(Dramatically)*: Because I'm a thespian.

JOSÉ #1: A lesbian?

HERBERT: No, I'm an actor.

(After a pause, the two Josés crack up. Herbert leaves the taco stand and walks into a dramatic pool of light. He performs a monologue from Richard Talavera's play Trial of los Siete.)

In Heaven. I'm in Heaven with Neanderthals, Samurai and wives. And, if I remember living, it's like having a small itch or humming something while you remember or forget something else. It doesn't really matter, because in Heaven, everyone is equal.

When I died, there was such an unraveling of consciousness. The sound of the gun exploding was suspended in time. Who was I when I was alive? A cop? A husband? Did I have children? I don't remember, it's very humiliating. I said to myself, "I'm an American." And, in that same precious instant, I asked, "What is an American?" I don't know. I don't remember.

The population of Heaven is young, brown and does not speak English. I have found very few "Americans" here. Everybody here seems to be Black, Latino, Arabic or Chinese. So, I guess Heaven is like Earth. And, the Mission was becoming more like Heaven everyday. But, I didn't see it that way; no, no, like the rest of us, I was blinded by prejudice and by fear. I guess I wasted a lifetime.

Everything I remember, everything I forget. The crickets at night, the socks under the bed, the way the sun shined on my grandfather's balding head creating a rainbow. And, if I could cry, I would cry ten lifetimes for the stones I used to skip, and more for the ones I kept in my pocket.

I guess I'm still unravelling all those things that I remember and all those things that are burning, burning into forget. *(Pause)* But, there are two words I remember when I was alive. They were . . .

JOSÉ #1 AND JOSÉ #2: YOU'RE FIRED!!!

(Blackout.)

SCENE SEVEN

The Auditions

Lights up. Richard walks into the light.

RICHARD: Hi, thank you for the audition. Yes, I just got the script, my Spanish is great. *(Holding product. With Anglo accent:)* Hola, su baño tiene mal olor? Es usted embarasado con sus visitas? No se preocupee-pee. Usted necesita "2000 Flushes." Deja su baño especta . . . culo, culo? Oh, espectáculo! Dísfrutalo, hoy!

(Blackout.
Lights up. Herbert, dressed like Frida Kahlo, stands in a spotlight.)

HERBERT: First of all, let me congratulate the producers at ABC-TV for doing the mini-series on "The Life and Times of Frida Kahlo." Excuse me? Am I willing to connect my eyebrows? For two grand, I'll make love to Diego Rivera!

(Blackout.
    Lights up. Ric does elaborate Bob Fosse-type dance. Lights black out in the middle of his dance.
    Lights up. Richard enters.)

RICHARD: I have prepared a song for the audition today. Here goes. *(Blows tune whistle. Sings:)* "Yo soy como el chile verde, Llorona, picante, pero sabroso . . ." What? You want it in English? Yes, I can do that.
    "I am tender chunks of pork in a light, zesty green sauce. Spicy. . . but not hot."

(Blackout.
    Lights up. Herbert is the sleepy Mexican, complete with sombrero, serape and cactus. He lifts his head slowly and points offstage.)

HERBERT: Señor . . . Indiana Jones went that way.

(Blackout.
    Lights up. Ric does a line from "La Bamba.")

RIC: Ritchie!

(Blackout.
    Lights up. Richard stares straight ahead; he holds a spear and speaks with his very best Shakespearean accent.)

RICHARD: Is it for fear to wet a widow's eye
That thou consum'st thyself in single life?
Ah! If thou issueless shalt hap to die
The world will wail thee like a makeless wife.
The world will be thy widow, and still weep
That thou no form of thee has left behind.

(Blackout. Richard continues in black.)

Look, what an unthrift in the world doth spend
Shifts but his place . . .
FUCK YOU!!!!

(Lights up. Herbert is Scarface/Tony Montana.)

HERBERT: OK, shut up! I said, shut up, cockroaches! Listen up, I'm a
very busy man! *(Takes out a baggie filled with cocaine)* What are
you looking at? I work hard for this shit. But, I have something
to tell you. *(Sniffs a huge amount of the white stuff; a large white
cloud forms)* I have coke here, and over here, *(Pulling can from
coat pocket)* I have new Diet Coke!

*(Blackout.
Lights up. Ric enters dressed as a giant taco.)*

RIC: Tired of those same old hamburgers? Eat me, eat me! Eat me!
I'm Taco Bell's new Taco Rancho Grande Olé! Just plop me in
your mouth and taste my delicious chile! So, whenever you're
in the mood for that south-of-the-border cuisine, remember:
(Singing to "La Cucaracha") El Taco Grande, El Taco Grande . . .
come and eat me while I'm hot. . . . El taco grande, el taco
grande . . . the next lines . . . I forgot.

*(Blackout.
During this blackout, we hear the sounds of Andean flute music.
Lights come up. Richard, Ric and Herbert are dressed in one serape and wear ridiculously long beards. Three separate holes in the
serape allow them to appear as a single three-headed body. They
carry a giant Andean flute and bob their heads up and down to
the tempo of the music.)*

HERBERT: Muy buenas noches. You soy Tito. You soy de Chile, huevón.
Que viva Chile, huevones! We are very happy you invited us
to the SerraMonte Ethnic Music Auditions. Thank you very
much. Que viva Chile, huevones!
RIC: Hola. Yo me llamo Jaime, soy de El Salvador. Oh, I love American womens and Grand Slam breakfasts at Denny's. If we win

the five hundred dollars for this audition, we feed the people of El Salvador. Que viva El Salvador, hijos de la gran puta!

RICHARD: My name is Jerry, I'm from Santa Cruz, what's goin' on? I was boogie-boardin' with my partners, Mad Dog and Snake, today, when I hit my head on a rock. I was in this blanket with these two Central American fuckers. It's really cool, now we're singing backup for Jackson Browne and Holly Near. Viva! Viva Los Lobos!

HERBERT: Que viva Chile, huevones!

RIC: Que Viva El Salvador!

RICHARD: Viva . . . uh . . . Paper Towels?

(Herbert ribs Richard.)

Ouch! We're really happy to be here and audition for you judges, 'cause we could really use the gig, man. We've been to about ten auditions today.

RIC: We want to win! We want to win!

RICHARD: So here is a special song we have prepared just for you all. Now, there is some controversy as to who wrote this song, but pay no never-mind. 'Cause we wrote it just for you. Ready, boys?

HERBERT AND RIC: Listos!

(The trio lip-synch to an a capella doo-wop version of "La Bamba." They exit and lights fade to a blackout. Music cross-fades back to Jerry Garcia's "Mission in the Rain.")

SCENE EIGHT

Mission Apartment

Lights fade up on the apartment. Richard and Herbert are still inside serape. Music fades out.

HERBERT: This is the last time I'm going on one of your stupid auditions! Andean trio my ass! And, why didn't we take this outfit off on the bus?

RICHARD: At least we got on with one fare.

(Ric enters wearing the giant taco outfit.)

RIC: What the fuck you guys lookin' at? All right, I got a callback to play a pinche taco.

RICHARD: Look on the bright side. Today a taco, tomorrow an enchilada. You work yourself up the food chain ladder. Next week you'll be a Chicken McNugget.

RIC: Maybe I should call upon the Grandfather Spirit . . . so he can find us more work.

HERBERT: Oh, great . . . are you saying the Grandfather Spirit is our agent now?

(Ric squawks at Herbert like a bird.)

RICHARD (*Reading a casting notice in a newspaper*): Hey, guys . . . the American Conservatory Theater is including a Hispanic play in their upcoming, prestigious season. How innovative of them! (*Reading*) A tall Hispanic actor is needed . . .

HERBERT: Bye, Ric.

RICHARD (*Reading*): Preferably with blond hair . . .

HERBERT: Bye, Herb.

RICHARD (*Reading*): . . . and blue eyes.

HERBERT: Hey, Rich, you got one blue eye, you should do it.

RICHARD: Herb, there's a theatre here looking for a balding Hispanic guy. The San Francisco Mime Troupe is looking for a black, feminist, politically correct, whale-watching actor of the Jewish faith.

(*Herbert opens up a bag of Doritos chips.*)

HERBERT: Dinner, anyone?

RICHARD: The Berkeley Rep is looking for highly intelligent actors to interpret overly symbolic magical realism. The entire run is already sold out by white, middle-class subscribers. Lincoln Center is doing an all-Latino version of *Oklahoma*. They are calling it *Choclahoma*.

RIC: That's it. I'm gonna kill a chicken for good luck. And, if that doesn't work, we'll have fajitas tonight.

RICHARD: Herb's right. We're washed up.

HERBERT (*Reading a Doritos bag*): Guys! I can't believe this. Guys! This is amazing. Maybe there is a Grandfather Spirit. Check this out. I am holding the future in my hands. Our destiny is on the back of this Doritos bag. Come here and read this.

(*Ric and Richard cross over to Herbert.*)

What's that say, Richard?

RICHARD (*Reading*): Stone-ground monosodium . . .

HERBERT: No, fool, here! (*Reading*) Doritos Chips, in association with the CBS Television Network, will broadcast live a world-premiere television special to celebrate the beatification of Father Junipero Serra.

RICHARD *(Grabbing bag, reading)*: Entire production to be filmed on location at the Mission Dolores in San Francisco, California. Genuine Costanoan Indians to be used for authentic atmosphere!

HERBERT: Oh, man. They're calling it the Camino Real Tour. And, guess who the guest star is? International singing sensation, Julio Iglesias!

RICHARD: Julio Iglesias! That's great, we can do the cholo skit!

HERBERT: This is it, guys. Our big break. We're perfect.

(Richard and Herbert begin to get hysterical at the possibility. They hop on chairs and begin to plan for their success. Horrified and offended, Ric backs up slowly to the upstage altar. Peyote music is heard.)

RIC: No! No! Don't you remember, guys? I was there with the Indios. *I was an Indio!*

RICHARD: Well then, you're a shoo-in for an extra.

(Apartment lights become dark and mysterious.)

RIC: No . . . I was telling you guys, I saw what Father Serra did, man. We're not going to perform, and for his canonization? We should canonize him with gunpowder! That's what we'll do. And, with Julio Iglesias? He's the great-great-great-great-great-great illegitimate bastard son of that bastard. No, we are not going to perform! No siree, Culture Clash will not lend its name to such an event, no siree, bucko! *(Let's out a loud bird call)* AAAAHH—ahahhh!

(Blackout.)

ACT TWO

The California Camino Real Tour Audition

House lights down. Lalo Guerrero's song "No Chicanos on TV" is played.

> I think that I shall never see
> Any Chicanos on TV
> It seems as though we don't exist
> And we're not ever even missed
> And yet we buy and buy their wares
> But no Chicanos anywhere
>
> The situation comedies
> The Jeffersons and the Cosbys
> Just change the channel and you get
> Arnold and Webster on the set
> They live with families of whites
> Not a Mexican in sight

There are Chicanos in real life
Doctors, lawyers, husbands, wives,
But all they show us on TV
Are illegal aliens as they flee
Or some gang member that they bust
Flat on his face, he's eating dust

Scriptwriters never write for us
I think it's time we made a fuss
Casting directors never call
They never think of us at all
Edward James Olmos and Montalbán
That's all we've got
Son of a gun

Don't buy the product if you see
There's no Chicanos on TV

Huggies has their three babies
White and black and Japanese
Chicano babies also pee
But they don't show them on TV.

(Lights come up. Richard, Ric and Herbert are seen in silhouette gearing up for the audition. They are dressed as homeboys complete with bandanas, pendleton shirts and baggy pants.)

VOICEOVER: OK, is the next group ready for the audition?

RICHARD, RIC AND HERBERT: Yes sir, we're ready!

VOICEOVER: We're an hour behind schedule. So you are Culture Club?

RICHARD, RIC AND HERBERT: Culture Clash!

VOICEOVER: Whatever. You have exactly five minutes to show us what you got. As you know, we are looking for that special Hispanic act for this upcoming Camino Real Tour with Mr. Julio Iglesias. Good luck. Go.

("Low Rider" by War is heard. Richard jumps into the light, followed by Herbert and then Ric. As soon as they begin their skit, the sound is turned off abruptly and the voiceover is heard.)

VOICEOVER: Thank you, guys, we've seen enough. Thanks again.

RIC: We haven't finished. We just started our skit.

VOICEOVER: Thank you. Next!

HERBERT: You don't understand. We worked real hard for this audition. Let us finish it.

VOICEOVER: I'm sure you have, but you guys are just not ready.

RICHARD: Ready, ready? What do you mean, not ready? I'm ready. I studied Shakespeare. I know . . .

VOICEOVER: Look, you guys just don't look Hispanic enough, you're too Chicano.

HERBERT: What do you want, mariachis?

VOICEOVER: OK, that does it. Security. Somebody call Security!

RIC: Go ahead, call Security! This isn't the last you've seen of us.

HERBERT: We're gonna get on that show one way or the other. Let's go, boys!

(Together they line up, back up slowly, snapping their fingers a la "West Side Story." The theme song to "Mission Impossible" is heard, and they dance out. Lights fade out.)

Spic Talk

As lights from the last scene fade, a video monitor begins playing a cheesy Hispanic talk show:

DICK MONTY: Welcome back to the program, *Spic Talk*. As you know, it's a very special show this afternoon. We're coming to you live from Mission Dolores in the heart of the Mission District. As everybody knows, we're kicking off the California Camino Real Tour, and to nobody's surprise, international singing sensation Julio Iglesias will be singing, and a very lucky Hispanic group will be opening up for Julio. There has been a statewide talent search to find that special act. And, in our studios today, a terrific friend and just a great man, himself— ladies and gentlemen, please welcome Mr. Julio Iglesias. Julio, thank you so much for taking time to come here on *Spic Talk*.

(Julio talks in a lispy Spanish accent like Father Serra.)

JULIO: Gracias, Dick. I am very happy to be here.

DICK MONTY: Julio, why a California tour?

JULIO: Because I love California. California has the finest beaches.

DICK MONTY: Bitches?

JULIO: No, beaches. Redondo Beach, Malibu Beach, Manhattan Beach. That's where I go skinny-dipping and get my Monte Carlo tan.

DICK MONTY: Julio, do you like living in America?

JULIO: I love America, Dick. America has given me so much . . . money. Vale, vale. They took me to the Statue of Liberty in

New York City, and you don't know the joy I felt to be inside of her. I was so happy I came . . . to America.

DICK MONTY: I read somewhere that you might be changing your name?

JULIO: Yes, now that California is "English only," I am changing my name to sell more records. I am translating my name to July Churches. Plácido Domingo already changed his name to Pleasant Sunday.

DICK MONTY: Well, Julio, how about singing us a song?

JULIO: Oh, si, con mucho gusto.

(Julio sings "Amor, Amor." In the middle of the song, three masked men kidnap Julio, live on TV, and exit with him. The TV goes to static, then to a cheesy Spanish weight-loss commercial. Towards the end of the commercial, Richard and Ric, wearing Mexican wrestling masks and carrying toy guns, come crashing into the apartment with a bound and gagged Julio Iglesias. They seat Julio center stage. Apartment lights go up. The video continues with Dick Monty back on again. Ric and Richard watch the video while Julio faces the audience.)

SCENE THREE

Mission Apartment

On video:

DICK MONTY: All hell has broken loose at Studio HH here on *Spic Talk*! Three masked terrorists have entered the studio and have kidnapped . . . I repeat, kidnapped, Julio Iglesias. And, you saw it here live on *Spic Talk*, and always remember to watch the show every Sunday morning at 5:30 A.M. Like I said, three masked terrorists made their way into the studio and they have demands. Thousands of horrified viewers have gathered outside the studio. The phones are lighting up. Can we get a shot of the fans outside the studio, Harry, can we get a shot?

(A video image of a large crowd waving "FREE JULIO" signs and chanting.)

One of the terrorists is here with us. Sir, we don't know who you are, we do not know your identity. Please tell us, what are your demands?

HERBERT *(In a Mexican wrestling mask)*: We have Julio Iglesias. But, first, cameraman, please, a tight shot of me, because I don't want to be in the same frame with this asshole! I am going to take my mask off because my identity will be revealed tomorrow, anyway. Guys, you can take your masks off, too.

(Ric and Richard take their masks off in the apartment.)

We have demands. We, Culture Clash, have abducted Julio Iglesias because we feel we represent all oppressed Latino artists. And, we will not release Julio Iglesias until Culture Clash performs tomorrow night at the California Camino Real show. After we perform and have been on national TV, we will release Julio, unharmed.

DICK MONTY: Well, there you have it. Live, here on *Spic Talk.*

HERBERT: I am not finished, Dick! I have more demands, and they are as follows: we want to arrive at the event in a limousine chauffeured by a white guy. And, backstage we want a kegger of Coors beer.

RICHARD *(Yelling at the TV)*: That's Corona, asshole!

HERBERT: Oh, I stand corrected. That's Corona. And, don't call me asshole, Richard. And also . . .

(On the video, handguns and rifles are suddenly pointed at Herbert. The TV goes to static.
Back at the apartment:)

RIC: Oh shit, they got Herbert!

(Richard turns off the TV and silently circles Julio.)

RICHARD: Julio, I hate your fucking Spanish guts! . . . Can I have your autograph?

RIC: Richard, can you believe we got Julio Iglesias here in our apartment. That's Julio Iglesias!

RICHARD: Let's hear the son of a bitch talk.

(Richard removes handkerchief from Julio's mouth.)

RIC: Habla Inglés?

JULIO *(Sings)*: Please release me, let me go. Indios salvajes. Hijos de puta! Do you know who I am?

RIC: Fernando Valenzuela?

RICHARD: Tony Orlando?

RIC: Charo?

RICHARD: Cheech?

RIC: Chong?

JULIO: Oh, very funny. Remind me to go see you perform in San Quentin prison! You better let me go. You'll never get away with this. Oh, I never been in the barrio. I should have never come to America. Look what happened to John Lennon.

(Ric and Richard re-gag Julio and move away from him to discuss their predicament.)

RIC: What if he's right?

RICHARD: What if Herbert got busted?

RIC: What if the FBI follows him here?

RICHARD: What if we get busted?

RIC: What if we go to jail?

RICHARD: What if I become a jailhouse bitch for the Mexican Mafia?

RIC: What if Cortez never conquered Mexico?

RICHARD: What if Malinche got a MacArthur genius grant?

RIC: What if Greg Brady boned Marsha?

RICHARD: What if Trotsky boned Frida?

(Ric and Richard continue to ramble on. Julio takes advantage of this opportunity and sneaks out of the apartment. Ric and Richard

realize this and freak out. They chase after him. Ric quickly returns with Richard, who is now bound and gagged. They realize their mistake and bolt out again. They come back with Julio and throw him on the couch.)

(*Angry*) I can hurt you!

JULIO: Wait! Stop! Look, if it's money you want I give it to you. No problem. Let me leave unharmed and I drop the charges.

RICHARD (*White-boy accent*): It goes deeper and farther than that, Julio. It's not about the money. It's about La Raza, La Gente, it's about La Comunidad!

JULIO (*To audience*): Oh, they're more stupid than I thought!

RIC: Hey, Richard, since when did you change your philosophy?

RICHARD: I was reading Carlos Casteneda's *The Teachings of Don Juan*, and I didn't understand a fucking word of it. And, that changed my whole philosophy of life.

RIC: Right on, Rich, I think. Julio, you are the modern-day Junipero Serra. You are a cultural imperialist. You take from la gente and you give nothing back to the community. We are the modern-day Costanoan Indians. We are going to claim our right to perform on any stage. The stage of life and the struggle of our people!

RICHARD: Viva Chicano Studies 101!

RIC: Que viva la Raza!

RICHARD: Viva Las Vegas.

(*Julio falls asleep and snores loudly.*)

RIC: It's just like Julio to fall asleep in the middle of my self-righteous Chicano dogma. Hey, I'll check the back door, Herb might come back through there.

RICHARD: Good idea. I'll keep an eye on Julio. I'll take first watch.

(*Richard sits next to Julio and pokes him to make sure he's asleep, blows in his ear, lifts his eyelid, etc. Then he curls up next to Julio like an infant.*

Julio's nightmare sequence: lights dim and eerie Native Amer-

ican music is heard. An Indio with mask enters, wakes Julio up, brings him center stage and flogs him. At first Julio's face shows pain, but then pain turns into masochistic pleasure. They both exit backstage.

Richard wakes up and talks directly to the stage manager.)

(Official) Excuse me, Todd, can you turn up dimmer five, please? Hi. I'm Richard Montoya of Culture Clash. My Anglo name is Dick. Can you say, "Hi, Dick"? Boy, you'll say anything. What we are doing right now is employing a simple Brechtian device: breaking down the fourth wall and talking directly to you, our audience. Herbert is backstage changing right now, we're kind of short on actors, the Ford Foundation money hasn't come through and we don't expect it to. Anyway, when Herbert comes crashing through the door, if you could just (a) act surprised, and (b) give him a round of applause. This will ensure a better night at the theatre, so really, the choice is yours. Now, I'm going back to "sleep." Just pretend we never talked. Todd, please take the light down. Remember, Viva la Raza! And, for our Jewish friends, Viva la Raza Shana! Good night.

(Herbert busts through the front door. Audience goes wild. Richard gives them the "OK" sign. Herbert embraces Richard.)

HERBERT: I'm back! Look! The milk carton already came out!

(Herbert holds up a milk carton with a picture of Julio and the word "missing" on it.)

RICHARD: We never thought you'd make it.
HERBERT: Yeah? How did I look on TV?
RICHARD: Like shit.
HERBERT: Where's Julio?
RICHARD: Right there on the couch.

(Herbert turns around and sees an empty couch.)

There. *(Hysterical)* Oh, my god! Where's Julio? *(Winks at the audience)*

HERBERT *(Panicked)*: You mean to tell me Julio was on that couch? You know what this means? He's escaped and he's at the police station, finking on us! We're gonna have the FBI, the CIA, the SPCA, and worst of all, Cagney and Lacey on our ass! Where the fuck is Julio?!!!

(Herbert starts strangling Richard. Ric appears from the bedroom door dressed in pajamas and a nightcap, carrying a teddy bear.)

RIC: Hey! Could you guys keep it down? Julio is trying to get some sleep. He had a bad nightmare.

HERBERT: Ricky, do you mean to tell me Julio is back there with you?

RIC: Yeah. Now keep it down, he's trying to take a nap before the big show. I'm reading him that Spanish classic.

HERBERT: *Don Quixote?*

RIC: No, *Ferdinand the Bull.*

(Ric exits. Herbert throws Richard to the couch in dramatic Spanish soap-opera fashion.)

HERBERT: Cabrona! Traicionera!

RICHARD: Déjame, bruto, bestia! Yo no sabía . . .

HERBERT: Cállate! *(To Ric)* Ricky!

(Ric reenters, dressed again in a terrorist costume.)

I want Julio out here at once. I want to talk to him!

RIC *(Indignant)*: We can't do that, Herb.

HERBERT: Why not?

RIC: Because that will be impossible.

HERBERT: Impossible? Ricky, I'm tired of your jokes. Get Julio out here now!

(Ric gives a nervous look to the audience.)

RIC: Herbert, we can't do it!

HERBERT: Give me one good reason why not!

RICHARD *(Sobbing)*: Because we need another actor, asshole!

HERBERT *(Realizing)* : Oh . . . Ricky! I want you to take second watch. I'll go back there and negotiate with Julio.

RICHARD *(Whimpering)*: What do you want me to do, Herbert?

HERBERT: I want you to go get some warm milk, some cookies, put on your pajamas, masturbate and go to bed.

RICHARD: Yes, sir.

(Ric kisses Richard good night on the cheek, and Richard exits. Herbert and Ric speak in cartoon gangster voices.)

HERBERT: Say, Ricky, you better not fall asleep, wise guy.

RIC: Naw. I'll keep my eyes wide open. Wide open, mugsy. *(Snores)*

HERBERT: Hey!

RIC: Ha, ha, just joking, boss.

HERBERT: Why, I oughta . . .

(Herbert exits. Ric sits, taking second watch.)

RIC: I can't believe it. We got Julio Iglesias here, in our apartment. Tomorrow's the big show. Man, we're going to be on national TV!

(Lights in the apartment fade down. A spotlight hits Ric. He pretends he's in front of millions of people.)

What am I going to do? I got to work on my material. And, now it's time for the one and only Slic Ric! I'll start off with my surefire stuff. Carnales y Carnalas . . . buenas nalgas! I used to have a lowrider with a bumper sticker that said, "Honk if you think this is your car." But, now I drive a Ford Fiesta, olé! And, it came with a special feature, three mariachis in the back.

My father is Juan Valdez and my mother is Rosarita . . . so as a kid, I was a hyper little fart. And as a kid, I used to watch this kiddie program *Romper Room* with Miss Nancy. And, she would say, "Romper stomper bomper doo, tell me tell me tell me true, magic mirror I see you. I see you John and Linda,

Kathy and Jennifer, I see you, Kevin, and I see you, romper stomper doo." You know all those years growing up as a kid and watching that show, that bitch never said my name once! Just once I would have liked to have heard: "Romper stomper bomper doo, tell me tell me tell me true, magic mirror I see you. I see Juan y Carlos, Margarita, Conchita, I see you Geesus. Oops! I mean Jesus. I see Wing Lao, Mohammed, Lattanya, and I see you too, Leroy, get down romper stomper doo!" Oh man, I am going to kill. (Long pause) Shit, we're gonna get caught.

(Blackout.)

California Camino Real Tour

Fanfare music is heard. Search lights are moving.

ANNOUNCER: Live from the beautiful Mission Dolores in the heart of San Francisco's Hispanic community, it's the California Camino Real Tour, starring international singing sensation

Julio Iglesias! And now, ladies and gentlemen, please welcome our first guests . . . *(Subdued)* Culture Clash.

("Lowrider" by War is heard. Richard walks in from stage left. He is dressed in a cholo outfit and carries a small radio. Herbert walks in from stage right, also dressed in a cholo outfit and carrying a medium-sized boombox. They greet and shake hands. Ric walks in from the audience dressed in a cholo outfit and carrying a gigantic ghetto blaster. He steps onstage, puts the radio down and does a comical handshake with Herbert and Richard, involving high fives, low fives, shoulder bumps, square-dance spins, etc. They all stop, give a triple high five, and each of them cops a pose. Music ends.)

RICHARD: Hey vatos, how come I always get the smallest radio? I'm going to get a pinche complex!

RIC: That's what your old lady said.

(Ric and Richard lunge at each other. Ric pulls out a giant butter knife. Richard retaliates with giant kitchen fork. Herbert stops them in their tracks.)

HERBERT: Stop forking around! *(Pause)* Carnitas!!

RICHARD: Carnitas?

HERBERT: I mean, carnales! This isn't a play about barrio warriors wasting their lives on the barrio streets of their minds, de chamberline, valentine, listen to my rhyme, tecate with lime, commit a crime and do the time.

RICHARD *(Feminine)*: I just love it when you get so macho.

RIC *(To Richard)*: Hey vato, whatever happened between you and your old lady?

RICHARD: My ruca wanted to get married.

HERBERT: That's a beautiful thing, ese.

RICHARD: I didn't like the vato she was going to marry.

HERBERT: Ah man, con todo cariño, con todo respeto, can I have her phone number so I can make a booty call?

RICHARD: Let me axe you something.

HERBERT: Axe me.

(Richard grabs a toy axe and chases Herbert around.)

RICHARD: Don't axe me shit.

RIC *(To Herbert)*: Hey vato. I haven't seen you in the barrio lately. Where have you been? Were you back in la pinta for parking tickets?

HERBERT: No, I've been going to Lamaze classes with my old lady.

RICHARD *(To Ric)*: Hey, Slic, I haven't seen you around the Mission, where have you been?

RIC: Well guys, I'm reformed. You see, I just got back from the Betty Ford Cholo Rehabilitation Clinic. I was there with Geraldo Rivera. The vato is a Huppie.

HERBERT: What's a Huppie?

RIC: You know, a Hispanic Yuppie. Hey, do you know the difference between a Yuppie and a Huppie?

HERBERT: No, what's the difference between a Huppie and a Yuppie, ese, vato, homeboy, carnal, vato loco, homeboy?

RIC: The difference between a Huppie and a Yuppie is . . . about $35,000 a year. *(To Richard)* Hey loco, where have you been?

RICHARD: I've been going to the opera.

HERBERT: Oh, that's the joint near San Quentin.

RICHARD: No, that's a prison. That's where I got these tattoos. *(He lifts up his shirt)*

HERBERT: Oooh. Care Bears.

RIC: . . . and Rainbow Brite.

RICHARD: Anyway, I was going to the opera, and just to mess with the white people, I pulled up next to this white Rolls Royce. I rolled down my window and axed, "Pardon me, ese, you got any Grey Poupon?" So, I got my Grey Poupon, my ruca, and went into the pinche opera. And in every opera they got a heroine.

(Herbert slaps his arm like a junkie.)

No, not that kind.

RIC *(Proudly)*: Just say no, just say no!

RICHARD: So this big heroine comes out stage right.

RIC: How big is she?

RICHARD: She can wear both of you vatos for earrings.

(Ric and Herbert pretend to be earrings.)

And, she's singing away . . . *(Soprano)* Fa la la la la, fa la la la laaaa. There's also a villain, a mean vato, and he comes singing stage left . . . *(Baritone)* Fa la la la la, fa la la la la la laaa. And in these operas there's a tenor, a fussy vato and he comes center stage singing, *(As tenor)* You can scratch my balls . . . *(As soprano)* I can't . . . *(As tenor)* You must . . . *(As soprano)* I can't . . . *(As tenor)* You must . . . *(As baritone)* I will!!

(Herbert picks up a chrome fender part from an old Chevy.)

HERBERT: Check this out, it's Freddy Fender.

RICHARD: Hey, don't ever touch that. It's part of Chuy's bumper to his ranfla. When I put this on my head, Chicano Magical Realism happens to me. We can have our own opera productions right here in the barrio. You don't need the Ford Foundation, just the Chevy one. Watcha, when I put this on my cabezón, I become an operatic character.

(Ric and Herbert put orange street cones on their heads and kneel.)

I am Chromodises, King of Chrome, boy lord of all lowriders.

RIC AND HERBERT: Oh, Chromio, oh, Chromio . . .

RICHARD: Wherefore thou art?

RIC AND HERBERT: Oh, Chromio, oh, Chromio.

RICHARD: Someone in the front row just cut a fart.

(They all begin playing with the cones.)

RIC *(Cone on his head)*: Look guys, "Surrender, Dorothy, he-he-he!"

RICHARD *(Cone on his nose)*: I'm Barry Manilow. "I write the songs that make the rucas cry."

HERBERT *(Cones on his arms and head)*: "Transformers, more than meets the eye."

RICHARD *(Cone on his ears)*: I'm the vato from Star Trek.

HERBERT: Yeah, Mr. Spic. I mean Spock.

RICHARD: "Beam me down, Scotty."

(Ric throws down dried pinto beans.)

I said beam me down, not frijoles!

RIC *(Cone on foot)*: Yo ho, yo ho, a pirate's life for me.

RICHARD *(Holding cone like torch)*: I am Lady Liberty, give me your meek, your huddled masses, just as long as they don't speak Spanish or win the Big Spin lottery.

HERBERT *(Phallic)*: Hey lady, here's your torch of liberty. Hey vatos, look, I'm a boy!

(Richard becomes nervous and tries to cover Herbert up. Ric grabs another cone and puts it between his legs, inverted. Richard gets even more nervous.)

RIC: Hey, I'm a girl!
RIC AND HERBERT: Boy meets girl!

(Herb inserts his cone into Ric's. Richard breaks them up.)

RICHARD: What's wrong with you vatos, what kind of an example are you setting for the Raza? You're not even having safe sex. You got on an IOU? You got on a diagram? I told you vatos to keep the aesthetic level high.
RIC: The Aztecs got high?
RICHARD: I'm not talking about the pinche Aztecs. I'm talking about fourteen million people watching us on national TV. I'm talking about my abuela and little children watching us. What the fuck's wrong with you vatos!?
RIC *(Interrupting)*: Hey, vatos, there's that gang from East Twenty-Second Street. Mad Dog!

(All three get close together and act like rabid dogs, barking and growling.)

HERBERT: There's those Iranians from 7-11.

(All three perform Iranian disco dance.)

HERBERT, RIC AND RICHARD *(Rapping)*: Colors, colors, colors, colors, colors . . . *(Singing)* De Colores, de colores se visten los vatos en la primavera.

Epilogue

Thunderous applause and cheering crowds are heard. Eerie music and police sirens heard under the cheering. The three guys move in normal speed—bowing, high-fiving, jumping and hugging. The eerie music takes over as the guys start to move in slow motion. Lights change.

The three form a huddle and move around in a ceremonial Native American circle. The eerie music changes to the Native American chants first heard in Act One. They break the circle and begin taking off their clothes until they are naked like Indios.

The three turn their backs to the audience and slowly raise their hands. They mime being arrested and have their mug shots taken standing in a jail line-up. Sound of a jail door slam. Jail bars light across the stage on them. As the three slowly exit, we begin to hear one verse of Lalo Guerrero's song "No Chicanos on TV." They continue to exit as lights and music fade out slowly.

A BOWL OF BEINGS

Photographs by Craig Schwartz

INTRODUCTION TO *A BOWL OF BEINGS*

by Richard Montoya

A *Bowl of Beings* was our Valentine card to the Chicano Movement. But it wasn't all about love and feeling good—there were healthy doses of rage, confusion, criticism, hope, despair and the eternal search for the perfect pizza. In *Bowl*, we play fellow travelers on a never-ending journey across a postmodern landscape littered with various pop icons of the last two decades, slaying a few sacred cows along our way. The Painted Bride in Philadelphia and ICM in Boston were just two of the alternative venues that we played, and they were cultural outposts as far as Chicanos were concerned.

After the success of *The Mission* at the Los Angeles Theatre Center a few years later, and the birth of an audience there that would continue to grow and support us, it seemed time to take *Bowl* to a new level. Once again we enlisted the help of director José Luis Valenzuela. Before we knew what the word, let alone the function, of a "dramaturg" was, José Luis was naturally acting in that capacity as we conceived and wrote a new and improved bowl of frijoles.

Around that time, Cheech Marin of Cheech and Chong bought us all tickets to see Cirque de Soleil at the Santa Monica Pier, and we met an Iranian-born genius director, the late Reza

Abdoh. These events and people would have enormous influence on the final work.

LATC was a cauldron of creative activity, not to mention a world-class venue for theatre. We were in the hot seat once again; we had to stand and deliver. Add to the mix Gronk (sets and costumes), José Lopez (lights), Mark Friedman (sound) and the fluid choreography and acting talents of Leticia Ybarra, and we had the recipe for one tasty pot of beans or frijoles de la olla. But there was another little matter that needed our collective attention first: the script.

There were aspects of the touring version that we were proud of and that could work for the new staging; however there were also many holes and gaps and the needed "transeeetions, mijos, transeeetions!" that were the shared obsession and hallmark of Valenzuela and the Clash. We had developed a keen sense of the cinematic, but now we were playing in the belly of the beast, the eye of the storm: Hollywood. This is where we sharpened our satirical fangs. We had seen one Hispanic group after another stage cheesy "showcases" for the industry, and we were damned well not going to do the same.

I remember standing on the roof of my prefab apartment complex in Hollywood on a hot summer day. We were plotting and planning the piece with Valenzuela. The Korean apartment manager of the complex had been murdered a few days before; her frail, tiny body had been found in a dumpster in the basement. Hollywood seemed a cold place on a scorching day; it was at once brutal, random, deadly and exciting. We were now writers in Babylon.

This new land served as our baptism into the dark. The fact that Columbus celebrations were already being planned for the quincentennial, the bloated and overblown decade of the Hispanic had just fizzled out, and we were still hungover from the alleged "feel-good-pick-yourself-up-by-the-bootstraps" attitude of the Reagan-Bush era (which wiped out many of the nation's not-for-profit art collectives) left us downright pissed, confused and full of rage against the fuckin' machine!

If there was a single incident that forced us on a decidedly spiritual quest, it would be the near-death experience of Salinas. Late one chilly night in the Mission District, following a Clash meeting, we all heard a vicious beating taking place and rushed outside. Salinas called out to the attackers to stop; then a faceless shooter pointed his shotgun at Salinas and pulled the trigger.

This incredible moment, frozen in time forever, had been prophesied to us by an Indian elder months before. The elder told us that our star was rising, that in fact we were Heyoka, or the Sacred Clowns. The symbol for Heyoka is the lightning bolt. The elder warned us that one must be very careful with this powerful symbol; lightning bolts can cause much damage, maim and kill. Careless, mean-spirited humor could do the same, he said. Was that the lightning bolt bursting out of the shotgun?

Salinas had faced his faceless would-be killer. It was now time for us to face the faceless, would-be killer of the Chicana/o movement, which had almost just died, too—thanks in no small part to increasing neoliberalism, conservatism, armchair reactionary revolutionaries and a growing number of Hispanics only too happy to once and for all bury the term Chicano. It was time to face the dragon and make carne asada out of him or her. I'm not saying we were responsible for reigniting the entire Chicana/o movement, but we played our small roles, giving birth to a renaissance on college campuses all over Aztlán (the Southwest). It reaffirmed for us once again the power of political theatre, that everything is political and that Diego Rivera was probably right in concluding that art and politics were inextricably connected.

We were also outsiders in L.A. (and still are). When you cut your teeth in places like La Peña in Berkeley, Victoria Rose on Valencia Street in San Francisco, the Guadalupe Cultural Center in San Antonio or the Galeria de la Raza—our birth place—when you are influenced by art collectives such as the Royal Chicano Air Force of Sacramento, you tend to fall back on these influences and take to heart the very tenets of activist Chicana/o arte, one of them being "la locura cura," or "craziness cures" (puro RCAF).

Life is short, as Salinas would say, full of surprises both good and bad. Death dances all around us. You may even find yourself dancing with La Muerte, having a cup of coffee or sharing a bowl of beings with him or her. That is a very Mexican sensibility; it's there in every José Guadalupe Posada print that came out of Mexico at the turn of the century and right through the Mexican Revolution. Funny thing was, we were wondering what happened to the Chicano Revolution or Movement, and what had happened wasn't very funny, or was it?

We needed a miracle; we needed Che Guevara to rise from the dead to shake things up and ask some necessary questions. Siguenza's mastery of mimicry suited him for the task of playing Guevara, but, more importantly, he had been to Havana on early "Brigades" of a cultural and political nature. Before we would assassinate Che yet again, this time in the urban jungle, we had to straighten out some shit, you know? Irony played no small part in our quest for answers that only unearthed more pinche questions!

The section of *Bowl* that is now being called "Chicano on the Storm" was our primal scream. It turned out many artists were feeling the same way. Our elders, our maestros from Dolores Huerta to José Montoya and Raúl "Tapón" Salinas, were right there for us, seeming to ask: What took you so long to figure out that Chicanismo is here to stay, and that our locura may be our saving grace? If you happened to be in the audience of one of those LATC shows, you felt it, you know what I mean. But you know, the words still seem to jump off the pages. We are still here. The struggle continues. Se puede? Sí, se puede! We can do it. Viva César Chávez! Viva la Virgen de Guadalupe! Y que viva Che! Next stop: sitcom hell.

PRODUCTION HISTORY

A Bowl of Beings received its premiere at the Los Angeles Theatre Center in June 1991 with the following cast and creative contributors:

Ensemble	Richard Montoya, Ric Salinas and Herbert Siguenza
La Muerte/Death	Lettie Ibarra
Voice	Alan Mandell
Director	José Luis Valenzuela
Sets and Costumes	Gronk
Lights	José López
Sound	Mark Friedman
Choreography	Lettie Ibarra
Stage Manager	David S. Franklin

LIST OF SCENES

The Ambassadors of Comedy
   La Vida Rap
   Nuestro Amor
   The Journey
Don Colón (The First Chicano Opera, 1492)
Ricflections
The Return of Che!
Chicano on the Storm
Stand and Deliver Pizza (The Last Chicano Movie, 1992)
Epilogue

The Ambassadors of Comedy

The stage is dark. Music and lights come up slowly. Richard, Ric and Herbert enter wearing trench coats, fedoras and sunglasses. The stage is a barren postmodern landscape with silhouette cutouts of human figures. A map of the Old World is painted on the floor. An ominous off-stage voice is heard:

VOICE: Where do they come from? What do they bring? Who are these ambassadors of Latino comedy and why am I speaking so dramatically? Not since Cortez toppled the Aztec Empire . . . not since Columbus discovered the Americas . . . not since Taco Bell introduced fifty-nine-cent tacos, has there been a force so powerful . . . so intense . . . so calculatingly Chingón!

Herbert Siguenza: an Aquarius. The mature one. The serious one. The potty trained one. Believes Culture Clash has succumbed to meaningless slapstick humor. Comedy is just a stepping stone to his ultimate goal . . . the Broadway stage! Oh, my, my, my, what a dreamer. Chicanos on Broadway—really now. Ha, ha, ha. What a loser.

"Slic" Ric Salinas: a Gemini. The heartbeat, the conscious, the wailing sphincter behind the group. An intellectual moron. Brown, but not too dark. "Así como café con leche." Translation: I won't tell you! Weaned on tortillas, frijoles and pop-tarts. Profile. Left. Right. Step back. He'll do anything I ask. He's my sex puppet! Ha, ha, ha!

Richard Montoya: penis. Son of a poet. Has been a Chicano since 1985. A Jewish comedian trapped inside a Chicano body. Was circumcised with a machete. Aspires to be a Santeriá witch doctor. He travels with live chickens . . . Chicano chickens . . . they lay eggs with the chorizo already inside.

And together they are—Culture Clash!

(The music abruptly changes to an instrumental hip-hop. Richard and Herbert dance as Ric raps.)

RIC:

We're back, as a matter of fact.
Clear the way, Jack, here's our plan of attack.
We state our case, we make our claim,
This ain't a game, we're not the same.
Pave the way, no time to play,
There's just too much we've gotta say,
No one can ever blow us away,
Culture Clash is here to stay.
We're here, we're there, we're everywhere
Now don't trip if we start to stare,
The paradox in life is clear
You're here today, you're gone tomorrow,
No need to fear
No need for sorrow
Live your life like there's no tomorrow
There is no need to beg, steal or borrow.
Live your life like there's no tomorrow.

La vida loca es para mí
La vida loca momma set me free
La vida loca for you and me
La vida loca that's the way it should be
La locura cura!

La vida tiene muchas sorpresas
Hoy feliz mañana tristeza
La vida es muy corta
Disfrútela eso es lo que importa
La vida es muy corta
Disfrútela eso es lo que importa y si no tienes suerte te va
    llevar la muerte.
Well my name is Ric
But you can call me Slic
And ya can't beat that with a piñata stick!

(A heart-shaped piñata lowers center stage. Ric swings at it and misses. Richard and Herbert taunt Ric to hit the piñata again. Ric breaks the piñata and the music changes to a mambo. A female dancer dressed as La Muerte (Death) appears and dances with all three of them. The song ends and she disappears.

    Los Panchos' "Nuestro Amor" is heard. La Muerte, wearing a silk shawl, reappears. Richard, Ric and Herbert now have suitcases. La Muerte gives one a blessing, one a hug and one a slap on the face. Then, she laughs wildly and exits. Richard, Ric and Herbert grab their suitcases and exit.)

Don Colón (The First Chicano Opera, 1492)

Opera music is heard. The set changes. Vinnie enters wearing a trench coat and fedora.

VINNIE *(Singing)*: The dark clouds of Spain are rolling over. There are lecherous ships out in the harbor. I must warn Papa. But, who am I? Only his illegitimate bastard son who sings opera on the side. My name is Vinnie. I have one blue eye!

(Ferdinand enters, wearing a trench coat. Music ends.)

FERDINAND *(Singing)*: I am Ferdinand, the noble son of Don Colón. There's my brother Vinnie, who has long hair. He looks as though he's in great despair. *(Speaking)* Yo Vinnie, how dare you sit in the Don's chair.

VINNIE *(Singing)*: Who is that that slaps me so? It's my Ethel Merman sounding bro. Ferdinand there's a murderous plot against Papa. We must warn him so.

FERDINAND *(Singing)*: You are speaking out of the side of your asshole.

VINNIE *(Singing)*: No Ferdinand, it is true! Fuck you!

FERDINAND *(Singing)*: Fuck you!

VINNIE *(Singing)*: No, fuck you!

FERDINAND *(Singing)*: Fuck you!

VINNIE *(Singing)*: They are taking Papa back to Spain.

FERDINAND *(Singing)*: They are taking Papa back to Spain?

VINNIE *(Singing)*: In chains!

FERDINAND *(Singing)*: In chains?

VINNIE *(Singing)*: Why do you repeat everything I say?

FERDINAND *(Singing)*: It's an operatic device! Fuck you!

VINNIE *(Singing)*: Fuck you!

FERDINAND *(Singing)*: Fuck you! Tu abuela!

(Don Colón—Christopher Columbus—enters.)

DON COLÓN *(Singing)*: I am Don Colón! *(He coughs, then speaks)* Fuck this, I'm talkin'. Boys, there are three vessels in the harbor ready to take us back to the Old World. The Rosarita, the Charo and the Maria Conchita Alonso. I am sure the King and Queen will reward me with a pension so I can retire. But what if I am asked to do yet another voyage? This I cannot do boys; I am old and tired. I want out of the shipping business, but they keep pulling me back in!

VINNIE *(Singing)*: Papa, may I speak frankly?

DON COLÓN: What is it, my little half-and-half?

VINNIE *(Singing)*: There is no coronation waiting.

FERDINAND: No coronation?

VINNIE: Opinions in Europe are vastly changing.

FERDINAND: Changing?

VINNIE: I hear there will be a hanging.

FERDINAND: A hangin'?

VINNIE *(Singing)*: Isabella and Ferdinand are pissed—the country of India you completely missed.

FERDINAND: Those fucking spics!

DON COLÓN: What? Do I have to prove myself again? Like my first voyage— *(He sits at his throne, picks up an orange and throws it stage right)* Sure, I didn't find any gold. I didn't find the passage to China. As a matter of fact, most of the time I didn't know where the fuck I was! Luckily I had my Thomas guide. But I did prove to them one thing! *(He catches an orange from stage left)* The world is round!

VINNIE *(Singing)*: Papa, my final warning—I must not allow you to board that ship.

FERDINAND *(Singing)*: Papa don't listen to him, he's full of shit. We must go!

VINNIE *(Singing)*: We must stay!

FERDINAND *(Singing)*: We must go!

VINNIE *(Singing)*: We must stay.

DON COLÓN: Shut up, both of youse. I have listened to both of my sons. I will contemplate this decision alone. New business!

VINNIE *(Singing)*: Pops, there is an Indian woman outside waiting to see you. Perhaps Ferdinand could open the door.

FERDINAND *(Singing)*: It's some Indian broad, named America.

DON COLÓN: America? The beautiful? Send the bimbo in.

(Ferdinand brings in America, who carries a baby bundle.)

AMERICA: Don Colón, buenos dias. Thank you for seeing me. I bring before you my only son. The last son of Chief Anacaona.

FERDINAND & VINNIE *(Singing salsa-style)*: Anacaona, India de raza cautiva, Anacaona—

DON COLÓN: Shut up! Please continue.

AMERICA: Don Colón, I beg of you, please give him your blessing.

DON COLÓN: You want me to bless the surviving son of Chief Anacaona?

FERDINAND & VINNIE *(Singing salsa-style)*: Anacaona, India de raza cautiva—

DON COLÓN: Shut up! I killed Chief Ana . . . his father. *(Realizing; to audience)* Whew! I almost said Anacaona again!

FERDINAND & VINNIE *(Singing)*: Anacaona—

DON COLÓN: Shut up! You want me to dip that bean? No way José, when he grows up to be an Indian activist he'll want to rip my heart out. He'll want to free Leonard Peltier and worse. He'll want to avenge his father's death. He'll boycott my quincentennial celebration. That's bad business.

AMERICA: No Don Colón! Please, not this child! He's weak. I'll make sure he grows up to be a nice little Indian and celebrates Columbus Day. He won't make any trouble, I promise.

DON COLÓN: No dice! I'm going to ask you to give over the little tonto to my son Ferdinand for proper disposal.

AMERICA: No, I can't let you! No, leave my baby alone!

(Ferdinand and America wrestle. The bundle falls, revealing not a baby but a large knife.)

FERDINAND: There is no baby, she's got a ginsu knife!

(America picks up the knife and threatens Don Colón.)

AMERICA: We were here long before the vessels of death arrived. You will pay for bringing genocide, disease and slavery to our peaceful people. You murdered, plundered and raped under the guise of Christianity. Prepare to die, you dog!

(She lunges at Don Colón but is shot by Ferdinand. She falls to the floor.)

FERDINAND *(Sympathetic)*: What a beautiful speech.

DON COLÓN: What!?

FERDINAND: Oh . . . I mean. . . . That was a close one, Pops; I got her right between the eyes. Hey Vinnie, how come youse just stood there, and didn't do nuttin'?

DON COLÓN: Why didn't you defend my honor, son?

VINNIE *(Singing)*: Because . . . because . . . she is my mother!

FERDINAND: His mutha?

VINNIE *(Singing)*: You killed my mama mía. Please don't let her die. She's my only Mom. Please don't let her die. *(Spoken)* I am *confused and full of rage.*

DON COLÓN: Vinnie, I'm sorry it came to this, son. Maybe you should just forget about your Indian past.

VINNIE: Never!!

DON COLÓN: Oh Vinnie, I know, you're confused, you're full of rage. But then again, you're history's first . . . Chicano!

VINNIE: Aaagh . . .

FERDINAND: A Chicano?!

DON COLÓN *(To Vinnie)*: Now act like a man and bury your Mama America. But first take her over to Enzo the mortician, make her look real pretty for those Indian powwows they have— oooh oooh. Ferdinand . . . now you know about your brother. I should have never gotten involved with America—but . . . she was virgin territory—because now I have created a monster—

DON COLÓN & FERDINAND: A CHICANO!!!

(Don Colón takes Ferdinand to the side.)

DON COLÓN *(Secretive)*: Ferdinand, you're my true blue son. I want you to take over my shipping business. Vinnie's just gonna get in your way. Comprendes Mendez?

FERDINAND: Give me the order, Pops. Give me the order!

DON COLÓN: Roast beef on rye . . . just a joke you idiot. Come here.

(Don Colón whispers an order to Ferdinand. Ferdinand pulls a variety of items from his coat: a slingshot . . . dynamite . . . a scud missile . . . and finally settles on a gun. Ferdinand approaches Vinnie and is about to shoot him when America sits up and stabs Ferdinand, then falls back, dead.)

VINNIE: Look what you have done Don Colón. You raped and mur- dered my mother America. And you hire my brother to assas- sinate me. Do you think I could allow this to happen Don

Colón? *(Yelling)* Have you no mercy? Have you no compassion? Have you no huevos?

DON COLÓN: Horseshit! Cut the dramatics, Vinnie. You're no Plácido Domingo, son. But, don't take it so personal. Business is business.

VINNIE: You will eat your words, Don Colón. One day my people will populate this new world. We'll own legitimate businesses. One day a dark little Indian will sit on the county board of supervisors . . .

DON COLÓN: No!

VINNIE: Yes, yes. Your time has come, Don Colón. I am the nuevo hombre, a product of two worlds. And, I have no idea why I'm speaking in an English accent. I know now what I must do. . . . Would you like a cannoli?

(Vinnie grabs Ferdinand's gun and points it at Don Colón.)

DON COLÓN: Vinnie, put the gun down. *(Confident)* What are you going to do, shoot me? The great explorer? You and I both know we cannot rewrite history—I didn't die this way, you fool. Ha, ha!

VINNIE: Well, Pops, let's just say this is more symbolic than factual. This is for five hundred years of genocide. *(He shoots)* This is for all Native Americans. *(He fires)* This is for La Raza. *(He shoots)* This is for Fernando Valenzuela. *(He shoots)*

(Don Colón falls dead.)

DON COLÓN: OK. I'm dead already. My wig fell off and I can't get up.

VINNIE: Happy Columbus Day, Papá. *(Overly dramatic)* Oh! Look, look what I have done!

(Vinnie drops the gun and slowly sits on his father's throne. "The Godfather" theme is heard. Lights, sound and set change. Native American flute music is heard. Ric, carrying a suitcase, enters.)

████████████████████████████████████

Ricflections

RIC: Grandfather. Hey Abuelo. I was about five when I first remember you, mi abuelo. You would take your white handkerchief, grab the tips, roll it in the air and then chase me, and at the right moment you would snap my butt. And, damn it would hurt. But you know something, mi abuelo, I loved every minute of it. Papa Wenceslao. He was about seventy-two years old then. Wenceslao. How the hell did he get that name? He first married when he was fifty, my grandma was thirty. Sly, huh? He was an atheist, vegetarian, dark-complexioned Indio with silver-white hair. He always wore a suit and tie, even to picnics. And he had this gray fedora. He looked like a Latino George Raft. He died when he was ninety-three, back in 1978.

Well, about a year ago I saw him again. In the hospital. I was laid out pretty bad. I felt his presence; I know he was there with me. I was in the intensive care unit for about a week. We were having a Culture Clash meeting at my house in the Mission District of San Francisco when we heard a disturbance out front. We went to check out what was happening. There was a kid getting beat up by a gang. They were beating him up real bad. I said, "Hey, he's had enough, let him go." I didn't even get in between them. Well it was dark outside, but I could see from about twelve feet away there was someone in a trench coat. He pulled out a sawed-off shotgun, I saw a flash of light, and I was shot!

(Ric has a flashback as Richard and Herbert, dressed as doctors, rush in with a human figure lying on a hospital gurney. La Muerte dances on top of the gurney. Frantically, the doctors "operate" on the figure. The doctors finally sew him back up. La Muerte holds his heart up high.)

HOSPITAL ANNOUNCEMENT: La Muerte to the AIDS wing please, La Muerte to the AIDS wing.

(Everyone but Ric exits.)

RIC: The gunshot blast caused my lungs to collapse. I was shot in my liver, I was shot in the colon, and I was shot in my heart. It was a seven-hour operation.

(Music ends.)

It happened so fast. I got shot and I couldn't believe it. I kept shouting: "I got shot! I got shot! I got shot!" It was like a movie. But then, it became real. So real that it became larger than life. It's hard to describe how my life flashed in front of me. It was more like a feeling. I remember my life, just slipping away. Yet a feeling more intense than I've ever felt. Each breath, I thought, was my last. I felt my life leaving me slowly, gently, delicately. I remember thinking that I was going to go into a deep sleep and find out what the fuck was on the other side. I mean I was right there on the edge. Then I yelled out, "Don't tell my mother!" Could you believe that? It was like when I was a little boy and I broke that expensive vase. Don't tell my mama. Everything was so three-dimensional. My mind began to work frantically fast. It was the epitome of panic. But this is what I think saved my life. I got angry, I felt ripped off. You mean this is the way I'm gonna leave this place? This isn't the way it's supposed to be. I'm not ready to go! I mean, one minute I was planning how we were going to come to L.A. and make people laugh, *(Pause)* and the next minute some motherfucking gang member blows me away! He turned out to be seventeen years old—seventeen years old. A kid with a big gun.

To this day, I don't know why, I never felt vengeful. In a way I feel sorry for him and so many others like him. There's a bigger picture out there. But hey, talking to you is like therapy to me. Can you blame me? It's cheaper than seeing a shrink. Well, I've been going to a doctor—not even a doctor, I get to see a surgeon. And my surgeon says that I'm eighty-five percent all there. Well, last year I asked him if it was OK to get back with the guys and he said, "Whatever makes you happy." And this makes me happy. So here I am, *(Like a broken record)* eighty-five percent, eighty-five percent, eighty-five percent . . .

But you know what really made me angry that night? I had just bought a brand-new, expensive Calvin Klein shirt. That really hurt. The guys kid around with me now. Whenever I lag behind they yell, "Hey Ric, get the lead out." But I look at the bright side of things; now I can drink all the beer I want and not get drunk, 'cause when I drink beer it all pours out of me.

After I got shot I was knocked to the ground and my homeboy Richard was right above me. He said, "Ric, buddy, is there anything I could do for you?" "Rich," I said, "Call 911." He said, "OK! What's the number?" Meanwhile death is ready to dance the mambo with me, right?

I know I got a second chance on life, and I don't take life for granted. And, I know this may sound corny but what the hell . . .

Enjoy life, respect yourselves, respect your loved ones, love your neighbors, a good hug now and then. Stop the violence; it's as simple as that. Bueno pues, tómenlo suave. *(He starts to leave and then stops)*

Hey Abuelo, it was good to see you again, thanks for being there. My doctor says I'm eighty-five percent now . . . chingao, I wonder where the fifteen percent went?

"In beauty may I walk. In beauty before me may I walk. In beauty behind me may I walk. In beauty above me may I walk. And in old age, wandering in a trail of beauty, lively may I walk. And in old age, wandering in a trail of beauty, living again may I walk. It is finished in beauty. It is finished in beauty."

(Carlos Santana's "Europa (Earth's Cry Heaven's Smile)" is heard. Herbert, dressed as Santana, enters. La Muerte, dressed as a ballerina, enters and dances with Ric. They fall to the floor and make love. He pulls away and as he exits, he notices Santana playing guitar. Ric gives Santana the thumbs-up. Blackout.)

The Return of Che!

A Cuban folk song about Ernesto Che Guevara is heard. A huge red and black banner of Che flies in. The setting is changed into a small Berkeley apartment. Chuy, a Berkeley Chicano activist in baggy clothes, enters. He picks up the phone and dials. Music fades out.

CHUY *(Into the phone):* Obviously you haven't been listening to me carnal, ese, I already told you, aye. I can't make it to the U.S. out of East L.A. Rally, homes. Because I'm busy that day, ese. Something heavy is coming down for La Raza that day. Something that is going to have impact on La Comunidad, ese. *(Pause)* The Forty-Niners are playing!

Excuse me, homes, don't ever question my commitment to La Raza. I've been a Chicano longer than you have, since 1985. I stopped in '90, but then I started again in '92. When's the next collectiva, man? I'll come to the next meeting. Oh, wow, Tuesday night? That's *N.Y.P.D. Blue* night, ain't it? Jimmy Smits going to show his nalgotas again? Brother's got a fine ol' ass, huh? . . . No, man, my old lady likes it. She thinks he's fine . . . not me, ese. . . . Hey, man, don't be homophobic. . . . Silence equals death. . . . And, so do your Pedos! I'll make it up to you vatos. I'm gonna put up flyers for the sensitive Chilean lesbian poetry festival. OK, I'll see you on the rebound, carnal. Oralé, simón. Uh-huh, yea, uh-huh, yea, yea uh-huh. Viva La Raza, ese. Chicano power. Que viva la mujer! De Colores and shit! Power to the Native Americans. James Brown is free, pende-jo. Oralé. We shall overcome, carnal. Boycott everything, aye, everything toxic: lettuce . . . grapes . . . strawberries . . . just say no. Hey ese . . . boycott your culo! *(He slams down the phone)*

Chingao. Being an activist in the '90s is going to be more difficult than I thought. There's not too many of us radicals left anymore. Chingao. What happened to the revolution? What ever happened to The Artist Formerly Known as

Prince? Chingao! What happened to El Movimiento?! The decade of the Hispanic turned out to be a weekend sponsored by Coors. What are we going to leave to the chavalitos besides Nintendo? No entiendo. How are we going to get back Aztlán? The only way to get our land back is the way Che did it. Total liberation through armed revolution. Que viva Che! *(Realizing)* Chingao, I'm missing the game!

(Chuy turns on the television with a remote.)

SPORTS ANNOUNCER: San Francisco versus the Los Angeles Raiders, Montana to throw—ooh he gets sacked!

(Chuy picks up the phone and orders a pizza from Domino's as he takes a hit off a joint.)

CHUY: Hey, is this Domino's pizza? I'm gonna be getting the munchies pretty soon . . . aye . . . pepperoni with extra cheese, yeah. No, no jalapeños, I'm boycotting those this week. Tell Frankie to bring my pizza; I like that crazy vato.

(Chuy hangs up the phone. There is a knock at the door.)

Damn, that was fast! Come in, the door is open.

(Enter Juan Santero dressed as a Caribbean witch doctor, all in white with necklaces around his neck. He comes in singing.)

JUAN: Tu me heciste, Santería. . . . eh Chuy, como está brother? Come está negro?

CHUY: It's Juan Santero!

JUAN: Dame un abrazo coño. Give me a hug.

(They hug.)

Hey Chuy, how do you like the way I look? I just got my Santería kit today. I called 1-800-VOODOO! Coño. Tonight we are gonna dance una salsita caliente. *(Making sign of the cross)* Celia Cruz!

CHUY: You're going to take me bailando, homes? Yeah, I've been practicing my salsa steps all week. Check it out.

(Chuy tries to dance a salsa step but instead dances a slow oldies shuffle.)

JUAN: Chuy, Chuy, no! Mueve las nalgas, las nalgas! Shake your booty! *(Pause)* At least you're better than white people.

CHUY: Hey, you just got back from Cuba! How's the music?

JUAN: La música como siempre esta chevere, pero se dice "Coobah," not "Cue-bah."

CHUY: "Ex-cooos-me!" Hey, homes, how's the revolution down there? I mean Fidel hasn't sold out, has he?

JUAN: No, Chico, Fidel is like a mountain that cannot be moved. In fact, in over thirty-nine years, he hasn't changed his philosophy or his fatigues.

CHUY: I am amazed by that vato. He's been governing those gentes for almost forty years and has escaped endless assassination attempts. He reminds me of Joe Montana on the five-yard line. How does he do it?

JUAN: He's protected by the "Orichas."

(There is a sound effect of wind chimes as both men look up. Chuy looks cross-eyed at his joint.)

He is protected by voodoo dolls given to him by a high priest-
ess of Santería, Santería, Santería.

*(Juan goes into a brief voodoo trance. Chuy looks at this joint
again.)*

CHUY: Dolls? You mean like Barbie and her old man Ken without
a dick?

JUAN: No. Dolls with spiritual powers. Like this one. *(He pulls a
black doll from a sack)* I brought this back from the Voodoo
Expo Show in Havana.

CHUY: I hate to tell you this, homes . . . but that's a Whitney
Houston doll!

JUAN: No coño! You are making me very angry, Chuy. This is a real
powerful doll. It can do anything to anybody, living . . . or dead.

CHUY: Puro pedo homes, it's just a muñeca.

JUAN: OK, Chuy, I'll prove it to you. Who or what do you want me
to empower?

(The sound of the football game is heard.)

SPORTS ANNOUNCER: Looks like the Forty-Niners are going to lose
this one. . . .

CHUY: Hey if you think the muñeca has magical powers, why don't
you help the Forty-Niners out? Montana looks like mierda!

JUAN: They're losing? Oh man, I bet fifty chickens on that game.
Hold this.

*(Juan hands Chuy a giant bone and puts two rubber chickens
around his neck. Voodoo music is heard. Juan begins doing ritualis-
tic chants and dance movements.)*

SPORTS ANNOUNCER: Looks like the Forty-Niners are going to lose
this one. San Francisco is down by three. It's fourth down, no
time-outs, they're at their own ten-yard line with only twelve
seconds on the clock. There's the snap. Montana to throw.
No, wait, he's going to run!

(Suddenly Juan makes the doll "become" Joe Montana and makes it run across the stage.)

He eludes one tackler, breaks another. This is amazing . . . he's at the fifty, the forty, the twenty, the ten. Touchdown! Touchdown! Forty-Niners! They win twenty-four to twenty-one! Joe Montana is doing the merengue in the end zone!

(Chuy and Juan perform a merengue victory dance.)

SPORTS ANNOUNCER: The white boy's got rhythm.

(Chuy turns off the television with the giant bone.)

CHUY: It works! It really works! Hey Juan, you were right. The doll really works!
JUAN: Te dije coño.

(Chuy looks at the Che banner behind him.)

CHUY: Hey, can you bring back the dead?
JUAN: Of course I can, Chuy, in fact last night I was playing babaloo with Desi Arnaz!
CHUY *(Desperate)*: Juan Santero, I have to borrow it bro. Give me the pinche muñeca!
JUAN: OK. I give you the doll, but you must remember this—a kiss is just a kiss. Ha, just joking. *(Preaching)* Whatever you ask for must come from el corazón, and it must be for the good of the people. And more important—may the fuerza be with you. OK, Chuy, I got to go. I have to go to a Santería Tupperware party. One more thing. Don't *fack* with history, man. Don't *fack* with history. OK, Chuy, I got to go now OK. *(He exits)*
CHUY *(Imitating Juan)*: I'll try not to *fack* with history, man. . . . OK, Janet Jackson, it's up to me and you. We've got to light the fires of radicalism. The Leftist movement needs a good shot in the arm. We've got Chicanos out in the suburbs driving

fancy cars—we've got beaners in beemers! OK, let's start the revolution, homegirl, bring him back alive . . . *(He begins to chant:)* Oye como va . . . got a black magic muñeca . . . *(But nothing happens. Angry:)* Chingao man, I have been fooled again by Juan Santero and his stupid tricks man, I can't believe I fell for it, that muñeca can't do nothing. *(He throws the doll through a slit in the Che banner. He picks up the phone and dials)* Hey, Juan? You're a phony, you're a fake, ese. The little negrita didn't do shit. I'm calling the Better Brujería Bureau! I never want to see you in my house again. Don't ever come over to my canton, man. . . . OK, I'll see you tonight. *(He hangs up and there is a knock on the door)* Must be my Domino's pizza! *(To offstage)* Come in, the door is open.

(Tango music is heard. A man dressed in fatigues and carrying a rifle magically comes through the slit of the banner. It is Ernesto Che Guevara. Chuy and Che stare at each other, dumbfounded. Chuy and Che tango for several steps, then stop abruptly.)

CHE *(Frightened)*: AAAHHH!
CHUY: AAAHHH!
CHE & CHUY: AAAHHH!

(Che points his rifle at Chuy. Music ends.)

CHE: Quien sos, vos?

(Che cocks his rifle.)

CHUY: Damn, Domino's does deliver!
CHE: Who are you?
CHUY: I can't believe it. Commandante Che, you're alive, you're alive, Commandante Che Guevara is alive!
CHE: Calláte pibe! Donde estoy? Where am I? The last thing I remember, I was in the mountains of Bolivia.
CHUY: Oh, man, wait till MEChA finds out. Commandante Che, I am Chuy. *(Holding the doll)* This is Juana La Cubana. A sus ordenes Commandante. *(He salutes)*
CHE: Sos Mexicano?
CHUY: No, Chicano.
CHE: Chicano? What is a Chicano?
CHUY: I don't know!
CHE: What country?
CHUY: Aztlán.
CHE: Que es Aztlán pibe?
CHUY: Aztlán is the land the Yankees stole from the Chicanos. It is Colorado, New Mexico, Texas, California, Arizona, a little bit of East L.A.
CHE: Ah! Los Estados Unidos! But where, compañero?
CHUY: Commandante, welcome to Berkeley.
CHE: Berkeley . . . macanudo!
CHUY: It's the last Communist stronghold in the whole pinche world. We're gonna have to get you some Birkenstocks . . .

(Che is confused.)

. . . just a little joke, Commandante.

CHUY: Commandante Che, I'd be honored if you were to sit in my Lazyboy.

(Che sits and takes out a cigar. Chuy gladly lights it.)

I have so many things to tell you, I don't know where to begin. Basically, you're dead.

CHE: What?!

CHUY: Commandante, they killed you in the mountains of Bolivia in 1967, and some say Fidel was involved.

CHE: What?! Nunca, never!

CHUY: I don't believe it either. But, these are the '90s, and with the help of Juan Santero and this little Oprah Winfrey doll, we brought you back from the dead, Commandante, because people have forgotten what you fought and died for. The Chicano movement is not moving. Chicanismo is on the way down; Stairmasters are on the way up. Come on, compañero, I've been waiting for this moment all my life. Sabes que Commandante? You got a rifle?

CHE: Sí.

CHUY: Pos, yo tambíen!

(Chuy pulls out an arsenal of semi-automatic weapons. Che is impressed.)

Let's take over city hall, then the police commission, and then we'll go down to Texas and take The Alamo!

(Chuy runs out but is stopped by Che.)

CHE: Idiota, wait! We cannot engage in guerrilla warfare at the present time. We need a strategic plan—I need to analyze your situation within its context. Compañero, first I will need a political and historical update since my death!

CHUY: Commandante, what luck, I have just the book right here: A Political and Historical Update Since the Death of Che.

CHE: Is it Russian?

CHUY: No, it's by James Michener, with a confusing foreword by Richard Rodriguez.

(Che is confused.)

Well, there's some good news and some bad news.

CHE: Tell me the good news.

CHUY: Bueno, Nicaragua had a Marxist government.

CHE: Que viva Nicaragua!

CHUY: But it was voted out of power.

CHE: Que malo.

CHUY: We also lost Czechoslovakia, Poland, Romania, Bulgaria.

CHE: Que? Bulgaria? What happened to Russia? The Communist party?

CHUY: The party's over, homes. Remember the Berlin Wall? Se calló, it fell down.

CHE: Se calló La Muralla de Berlin?

CHUY: Crumbled to the ground, Commandante.

CHE: Que horror! Esto no puede ser. Y La China?

CHUY: La China? The freak lives in Chinatown, want her pager number?

CHE: No, la China. Compañero Mao.

CHUY: Mao?

CHE: Mao.

CHUY: Mao?

CHE: Si, Mao. El Chino Gordo, pelón.

CHUY: Oh, I think he bought a trailer and moved to San Clemente. I think he was Richard Nixon's gardener. They sing opera on the side. Yeah, and now the government in China, homes, is on everybody's shit list because they killed a bunch of students in Times Square.

CHE: This is very confusing, compañero. . . . Tell me something, who won the Vietnam War?

CHUY: The Vietnamese.

CHE: Que viva!

CHUY: Then they moved to Orange County and San Jose.

CHE (*Frustrated*): Has the Left done anything since I died, compañero?

CHUY: Si, Commandante, the Left has made many strides since your death. Chile had a Marxist president.

CHE: Que bueno!

CHUY: But the CIA killed Allende in '73.

CHE: Que malo.

CHUY: Mandela is free.

CHE: Que bueno!

CHUY: But his old lady's locked up. . . . Grenada had a Marxist government.

CHE: Que bueno.

CHUY: But now it's a Club Med . . . special thanks to former president Ronald Reagan.

CHE (*Astounded*): Ronald Reagan? Ronald Reagan? Ronald Reagan fué presidente de Los Estados Unidos? Ronald Reagan, the "B" actor from Hollywood who made all those bad movies with that chimpanzee, *Bonzo Goes to Washington*?

CHUY: Yeah, except he left Bonzo at home and took Nancy to Washington!

CHE: Que locura! Who's your president now? A southern white liberal womanizer who smokes marijuana, plays the saxophone and goes white-water rafting?

(*Chuy gives a look to the audience.*)

CHUY: Commandante Che, these are crazy times. Communismo is on the way down, Starbucks Coffee is on the way up. But, I'm a little confused about one little fact myself, Commandante Che. When did you go out with Evita?

CHE (*Confused*): Evita Perón? I was a mere child when she was in power. Sounds like a Broadway musical.

CHUY: . . . or a movie with Madonna.

CHE (*Serious and dramatic*): What are you trying to tell me, compañero? That suddenly the spirit of "Internationalism" has died. That the philosophy and ideology of nuestros compañeros Marx and Lenin has faded? That Malcolm X was full of shit! That I died in the mountains of Bolivia, all in vain! *(He breaks down crying)*

CHUY: Ay Commandante! It's no reason to overact and spit all over the fascist subscribers in the front row. Commandante Che, you've got to pull yourself together, hombre. With all due respect you're acting like a pussy, homes.

Don't forget, you inspired a whole generation of yuppies, and besides, you made a handsome silk-screen poster . . .

CHE: What!?

CHUY: And you had some commercial impact, too.

CHE: Yo? Como?

CHUY: You know Carl's Jr. hamburgers?

CHE: Yes.

CHUY: Where do you think they got the "happy star" logo from?

(Chuy points at Che's famous star on his beret.)

CHE: NO!!!

(Che, in a fit of disgust, is about to shoot himself.)

CHUY: You can't do that, Commandante. You're already dead!

(There is a knock at the door. Frankie, the Domino's delivery boy, enters. Che runs for cover.)

FRANKIE: Yo Chuy, what's up, dog? Here's your funky fresh piece of melted cheese. I had them put some extra mozzarella on the motherfucker. Yo! Twenty-nine minutes and thirty seconds and I only hit three people. *(Notices Che)* Hey, who's the hippie?

CHUY: Hey, homes, have some respecto ay, I brought him back from the dead.

FRANKIE: The Dead? Hey, is that Jerry Garcia?

(Frankie takes out a lighter and flicks it on like a rock concert fan.)

CHUY: No, man, that's Che. Now, go shake his hand and show him some respecto.

FRANKIE: Yeah, yeah, yeah. Yo Che, Desert Storm, right?

(Frankie tries to give Che the Chicano handshake, but Che freaks out and points his gun at Frankie.)

CHUY: What's wrong with you, ese? The vato is dead, you could have pulled his arm off with that fancy shit! This vato's a revolutionary figure, Ernesto Che Guevara. He's a hero. Check this out. He would train guerrillas in the mountains, like Sigourney Weaver did, and the vato would come down into the little towns and overthrow the governments. He's a guerrilla in our mist. The vato was always on the side of the underdog, Frankie.

CHE: Bien dicho, compañero.

FRANKIE *(Not sure)*: Yeah? I think I read about him in Trivial Pursuit. On the side of the underdog, huh? Yo, man, sometimes I feel like I'm an underdog, delivering pizzas, getting minimum wage, having to walk over homeless people, in crack-infested areas. My girlfriend, she's pregnant, but I only owe six thousand bucks on my Mazda mini-truck. But you know, me and some of the vatos were thinking of calling a strike for better wages and shit. But we don't know how 'cause, well, *we're confused and full of rage.*

CHE: Compañero Frankie. You are the vanguard, the future. You remind me of Cue-bah.

CHUY & FRANKIE: Coo-bah.

CHE: Ex-scoos-me. Compañeros, let me demonstrate something very basic, compañeros.

(Che takes the Domino's pizza box away from Chuy. Pointing at the box:)

Dominos Pizza represents the Yankee oppressor.

FRANKIE: Yo, that's red, white and blue.

CHE: You are the oppressed worker, Frankie.

FRANKIE: No shit!

CHE: Together, we must, compañeros, crush the oppressor! *(He throws down the pizza box and stomps on it)*

CHUY: What the fuck! Che, that's my pizza!

(Chuy pushes Che off the box, sending Che across the stage. An angry Che points the gun at Chuy and Frankie, and they both stomp on the pizza box.)

CHE: Very good, you are learning! Compañeros, we must seize the means of production. I have a strategic plan. Frankie, we will overthrow your pizzeria, and then we will overthrow the entire franchise, and Domino's pizza will fall, one by one.
CHUY: That's brilliant.
FRANKIE: Yo man, that's live!
CHE: That's the Domino's Theory.

(They all give a look to the audience.)

(Urgently) Compañero, Frankie. Are you ready to struggle?
FRANKIE: I'm down!
CHE: Chuy, are you prepared to die?
CHUY *(Nodding yes)*: No.
CHE: Compañero Frankie, un grito por la liberación.
FRANKIE: Hey, Macarena!

(Frankie starts to dance. Chuy slaps Frankie upside the head.)

CHE *(Singing)*: El pueblo unido jamás, será vencido, the people united will never be defeated!

(Che and Frankie march around the apartment.)

ALL *(Singing)*: Compañeros comunistas, compañeros de la revolución.

(Che and Frankie exit with weapons. Chuy remains behind.)

CHUY: Compañeros, I'll be right there! I've got to prepare myself for the revolution. I'm gonna do some push-ups, make sure I'm ready, 'cause I'll probably be the first one to go down when the chingasos start. Am I ready to die? That vato takes himself pretty seriously. Commandante! I'm right behind you! I'm just gonna watch the Forty-Niner highlights first. I'll be right there, Che. *(He sits on his Lazyboy chair, turns on the television and starts eating his crushed pizza)*

SPORTS ANNOUNCER: Well Joe, you won the game in the last seconds, but you broke three ribs, and it looks like you're out for the rest of the season . . . one second. . . . This just came in—two men tried to hold up a Domino's pizzeria minutes ago. One, dressed like Communist leader and Broadway star Che Guevara, was killed. The other, identified as Frank Lopez, escaped and was heard yelling he would overthrow Domino's pizzerias and Taco Bell and then take a run for the border. More news at eleven. Now, back to the Forty-Niner highlights . . .

(Chuy turns off the television.)

CHUY *(Upset)*: Chingao, what a bummer! I'm all sad and shit. *(Pause)* Joe Montana will be out for the whole pinche season.

(The Beatles' "Revolution" is heard. The lights slowly fade. The set changes. A psychiatrist's couch is placed center stage. Two doctors enter and remove Chuy's shirt, then put him in a straightjacket. Chuy is now Richard. The music changes to The Doors' "Riders on the Storm.")

Chicano on the Storm

RICHARD *(Singing)*:
> Chicanos on the storm.
> Chicanos on the storm.
> Into this house we're born.
> Into the stage we're thrown

Like a dog without a bone,
An artist without a grant
Chicanos on the storm. Yea . . .

(Enigma, played by La Muerte, enters. She is dressed as a nurse and carries a clipboard.)

RICHARD: Who are you?

ENIGMA: Enigma.

RICHARD: Who am I?

ENIGMA: Rico Suave.

RICHARD: Where am I?

ENIGMA: In the barrio streets of your mind, all chuckhole lined.

RICHARD: Why am I here?

ENIGMA: Because, silly, you're confused and full of rage. Now, let's take our medicine.

RICHARD: What's it for?

ENIGMA: It will make your penis larger.

RICHARD: What?

ENIGMA: Oh yes, bigger than Ric's and Herb's. Now just relax. Today is our Christopher Columbus two-for-one special. You may ramble on for an extra hour if you wish. The doctor is always listening. Have an extra-special visit.

RICHARD: Nursey?

ENIGMA: Did you have a question?

RICHARD: Yes nurse, my question is this: what is going to happen to the word "Chicano"?

ENIGMA: The word Chicano will be replaced in the '90s.

RICHARD: My God. With what?

ENIGMA: The new term is "Tropical Anal Mist."

RICHARD: I'm a tropical anal mist?

ENIGMA: Have a nice day.

(Richard lets out a primal scream. Dramatic music is heard under the following monologue.)

RICHARD: I'm crazy, I'm a crazy motherfucker, I'm loco in the cabeza. I'm your postmodern Mexican Hamburger Helper.

Brothers and sisters run, run for the hills—have you heard Madonna wants to play Frida Kahlo in a movie, man. I finally find myself a hero and she's gonna fuck it all up for me— I hope they let a Chicano play Trotsky at least. What the fuck are you looking at up there? Haven't you ever seen a multicultural nightmare coming unglued right before your very eyes, man? 'Cause I'm Spanish, I'm Indian— American Indian, a "Dances With Wolves" kind of Indian— ahooo!

I'm a walking, talking grantwriter's dream, baby. . . . Is that the L.A. Festival in my pocket or did I just cash my NEA check? Ignore the dents, ignore the critics, they don't understand my multipersonality multicultural ways. Hell, I don't even understand them and I wrote this shit during a commercial. I never read Kafka, I never read Tolstoy, I don't even know the words to "La Bamba"! I'm a Chicano trapped inside the Beverly Center and I can't get out. I'm tired of being whore for your laughter, I want your goddamned respect. I want you inside of me right this very moment—the inside of my stomach feels like a Marquez novel: *Love in the Time of Colorization*. So, I bought me one of those ninety-nine cent Virgen de Guadalupe candles the other day and the little virgin's got a price bar code attached to the bottom of her feet above the little angel—that little fellow that's held her up all these years now looks like a fucking zebra! So, I joined me one of those benevolent Hispanic organizations like MALDEF or LULAC; this one's called MOCOS. It stands for Mexicans or Chicanos or something. . . . We don't have any bylaws. We're just trying to keep our noses clean. We're trying to maintain our chile-eating ability.

(*Reflective*) I wanted to be white when I was a kid; I wanted to be white like this jacket. I wanted to be white like my little pal Joshua. . . . Man, that sucker was white! He had little purple veins popping out of his head. He was my little gringo trophy, he was. It wasn't that I was ashamed of who or what I was, no I was proud to be African-American. I wanted to be white for simple reasons, for disciplinary reasons. White kids never got whipped; we were always getting whipped at our house. My old man could drive a car, turn around and hit ten kids with one swipe. Boom! Boom! I went to kindergarten thinking my middle name was cabrón. Over at Joshua's house, his mother would always tell us to hush. Everybody hush. I love the sound of that word, but I never could grasp the concept, ya know, over at my house it was callate el hocico!!

If you said a cuss word at Joshua's house, his mother would wash out your mouth with soap and water; if you said a cuss word at our house, you got your mouth washed out with jalapeños. After I got in trouble at my house, I would run to Joshua's, call his mom a puta just to get a soapy rinse job. I never understood the bedtime stories we were told as kids neither. Like most kids we would get tucked in and say our prayers, but here's where the story differs. Then our aunt, with no teeth and a moustache, would come in the room and proceed to tell us the wonderful bedtime story of "La Llorona"! La Llorona killed five children in their sleep.

"Mijo, tonight I'm going to tell you about La Llorona. Esa muchacha took her little mocosos down to the river and she drowned the cabrones. Ay que fuerte la mujer Mexicana.

Now you go to bed, mijo. Sweet dreams, mijito. Don't forget to pray to La Virgen and don't forget about La Llorona." Then they wondered why we peed the bed at night.

The Virgin of Guadalupe and La Llorona, great role models for my sister to shoot for. Of course now that I'm a feminist, I understand that La Llorona was simply a victim of her abusive husband, El Coocui. El Coocui is that bogeyman that lurks underneath everyone's bed. Every culture has got their very own version of El Coocui. Oh my god! There's one right there, it looks just like Daryl Gates.

Can you imagine La Llorona and El Coocui married under the same household? No wonder things fell apart. Things were competitive at home.

But there is documentary proof that El Coocui and La Llorona did seek out a marriage counselor to help pull their marriage back together again.

(As counselor) La Llorona, El Coocui, thank you for coming in the office. Today, we're gonna put all our angers right here on the table and find out what's troubling this happy marriage. La Llorona, you go first. I'd like you to share with us. What don't you like about your husband El Coocui?

(As La Llorona) He never spends any time with me anymore; he's always under the bed scaring the chavalitos.

(As El Coocui) I scare the children? At least I didn't drown half the sons of bitches!

(As counselor) La Llorona, El Coocui, let's just hush. We're gonna try something unorthodox to try and help pull your marriage back together again. We're gonna fly both of you down to Los Angeles, and you're gonna read love letters to each other at the Cannon Theatre. It's multicultural week over there. Don't worry, if it doesn't work out, we have understudies for you: Gloria Molina and Richard Alatorre. *(Los Angeles County Supervisors)*

La Llorona and El Coocui, the ultimate Chicano couple. We had a neighbor man on our block; he had a drinking problem, except he never did fess up to it. It became painfully evident as the years wore on. His eldest son was named Tecate, had a little daughter named Corona, the twins—Dos Equis. The little güerito—Bud Light, and his wife's name, La Margarita; she always had a ring of salt around her lips.

Actually, my parents were the ultimate Chicano couple. My daddy was from the mountains of New Mexico. Proud, strong and a little bit macho. My mom was the original Chicana Valley Girl, born in a mall I'm sure. I like to speculate on what their wedding night must have been like. My daddy was probably trying to test the macho waters a little bit: *(As Father)* "Mujer, I want you to make me some tortillas and frijoles and then fluff and fold each of my chonies . . ." *(As Mother)* "Aye dios mio. Mr. Macho wants me to make his tortillas and frijoles? Like, fuck you." *(As Father)* "Mujer, I'm only going to say this one time, mujer . . . *(Pleading)* Please don't leave me."

You know what made me different as a kid? I had one blue eye. I still got the sucker. People can be so cruel when you're different. They said I was the bastard son of El Coocui. Well, that's what my mother told me. I was a child prodigy of the Chicano movement, my instrument was my mouth.

One night, true story. César Chávez, presidente of the United Farmworkers of America, came to our house for dinner, an auspicious occasion. My mother cooked up all this incredible Mexican food with her own hands—homemade tortillas, beans, rice, tamales all laid out before him.

César didn't eat a thing. He was fasting that night. I recognized a window of opportunity, and I asked César if I could have his chile relleno. It was mistook as a sexual advance. I was sent to my room with no dinner. So, in solidarity with César, I fasted too. The Chicano movement ended for me the day my parents got a divorce. I remember my daddy pulling his Volkswagen van out of our driveway. My old man was César Chávez to me, he was Che Guevara, too. Come to think of it, he was always pissed off because our front lawn always looked like a jungle. Something happened to me that day though, strange as it was. I quit wanting to be white. I had finally come to grips and happily embraced my Japanese heritage.

(He picks up a harmonica and plays "De Colores") I dedicate

this song to El Movimiento and my parents. *(Plays)* Bob Dylan for the United Farmworkers. *(Sings like Bob Dylan)* De Colores, De Colores en los campos en la primavera. De Colores . . . *(Spoken)* All that discipline wasn't so bad, though. Last I checked with Joshua, he was doing fifteen to life at San Quentin, and I'm doing nonprofit theatre.

(Blackout.)

Stand and Deliver Pizza (The Last Chicano Movie, 1992)

Glen Miller's "In the Mood" is heard. A pachuco/zoot suiter struts in and snaps his fingers. The music stops.

PACHUCO/ZOOT SUITER: It was the secret fantasy of every vato in and out of the Pachuda to become . . . a math teacher.

(The pachuco snaps his fingers and music resumes. He makes a quick costume change onstage and transforms into Jaime Escalante, the math teacher from Stand and Deliver.)

JAIME ESCALANTE: The story I am about to tell you is about two pendejos who were into gangbanging and PCP instead of $E=mc^2$. Órale, con safos, vámonos.

(Escalante snaps his fingers and hard rock music is heard. A cholo homeboy from the barrio and a longhaired rocker enter from opposite sides of the stage. The cholo and rocker fight furiously until Escalante snaps his fingers and freezes them. The music stops.)

JAIME ESCALANTE: Órale gallos! What a waste of pinche time, no gente? Look at the cholo with his shiny calcos . . . twin mirrors of despair, look at his nethead, holding his greasy hair.

Looks like Spiderman. Look at the rocker with his tight puto jeans, makes his ass look like an apricot, que no? After teaching math at an East L.A. high school, I decided to open up my own business, y que! But I wanted to continue to help helpless mocosos like these become good working citizens. So relax, and enjoy the pretense. This is the story of "Stand and Deliver, Pizza!" Que la chingada!

(Escalante snaps his finger, unfreezing them. The set changes into a pizza stand. A giant pizza slice is lowered in the background.)

CHOLO *(Rapidly)*: Hey. Mr. Escalante. I hear you need somebody to make and deliver pizza three P.M. to midnight, Monday through Friday órale con safos, ese, vato, carnal, loco homeboy.

JAIME ESCALANTE: Órale, don't try to out-Pachuco me, ese. Do you know how to read?

CHOLO: No.

JAIME ESCALANTE: Did you graduate from high school?

CHOLO: No.

JAIME ESCALANTE: Do you know how to count?

CHOLO: Yeah. One, two. *(He extends middle finger)* Tu abuela!

JAIME ESCALANTE: Wise ass, huh? I bet you don't even know who Shakespeare was?

CHOLO: I kiss thy fair maiden as the cygnets flow in the ebb of night.

JAIME ESCALANTE: Órale. That's good. Is that from *Richard the Third*?

CHOLO: No, *Two Vatos from Verona*.

JAIME ESCALANTE: Oh, yes. Do you have a lowrider?

CHOLO: Yeah.

JAIME ESCALANTE: Do you have the ganas?

CHOLO: Gray hair?

JAIME ESCALANTE: Not canas—ganas!

CHOLO: Simón.

JAIME ESCALANTE: Órale, you got the job. Let's make pizza!

(Escalante snaps his fingers. Hard rock music is heard. Escalante and Cholo mime making pizza. Music fades.)

ROCKER: Hey, dude. I got the fucking munchies so hurry it up. Give me a burrito.

JAIME ESCALANTE: This is a pizza place—Cholo, make him a piece.

ROCKER: Ah, man, look at who they got working here. It's the cholo loser! Hey, I don't want him making my piece of pizza. He'll probably put some jalapeños on it, man.

CHOLO: Don't mess with me, coconut. I just got this job and I don't want to blow it, aye.

ROCKER: Oh shut up, you jalapeño-eating, lettuce-picking, para bailar la bamba loser.

CHOLO: Órale, that's it, Rocker, you die.

(They start to fight. A blast of hard rock music is heard. Escalante snaps his finger, and they freeze. Music stops.)

JAIME ESCALANTE: You see, gente. Two pendejos going after each other's throats over a melted piece of mozzarella. Two brown brothers, different from each other. But both not seeing the reality of their own ignorance. Ignorance breeds violence, violence breeds ignorance, and ignorance breeds Republicans!

(Rocker unfreezes.)

ROCKER: Yeah, and Republicans make long speeches. Hurry up, asshole!

(Cholo unfreezes.)

CHOLO: Yeah, Kimo. My arms are getting very, very tired!

(Cholo and Rocker freeze themselves.)

JAIME ESCALANTE: OK, OK. What these vatos need is someone who will believe in them again. Someone who will give them a second chansa. Someone who's out of their pinche mind. Like me.

(He unfreezes them with a snap.)

CHOLO: You lucky he froze us, Rocker.
ROCKER: Yeah, well I would have kicked your ass, Cholo.
JAIME ESCALANTE: Cool it, guys.
CHOLO: Yeah right, coconut.
ROCKER: Chicano.
CHOLO: Surfer.
ROCKER: You Los Tigres del Norte eight-track tape listener.
CHOLO: You 7-11 Slurpee, Guns N' Roses, MTV, white boy wanna-be.
ROCKER: Lowrider.
CHOLO: Gringo.
ROCKER: Greaser.
CHOLO: Honky.

ROCKER: Hispanic.

CHOLO & JAIME ESCALANTE *(Shocked)*: Hispanic!?

(Escalante breaks them apart.)

JAIME ESCALANTE: Órale, calmantes, monte patas chicas! Enough of this pedo. You're going to respect this place, like the world and live in peace and harmony! Rocker, I'm gonna give you a job.

ROCKER: Excellent, Kimo.

JAIME ESCALANTE: I'm starting you at $2.50 an hour.

ROCKER: That's bogus, Kimo.

JAIME ESCALANTE *(Sly)*: OK, $7.25 a day.

(Rocker does calculation with his hand.)

ROCKER: Sounds killer.

JAIME ESCALANTE: Great. Now you work together, shake hands.

(Reluctantly they shake hands.)

(Orders) Chicano handshake.

ROCKER: I might not know it.

JAIME ESCALANTE: Yes, you do.

(They do the Chicano handshake.)

JAIME ESCALANTE: Say you're sorry.

ROCKER: Aw, come on.

ROCKER *(Simultaneous with Cholo)*: Sorry, Cholo

CHOLO *(Simultaneous with Rocker)*: Sorry, Rocker.

JAIME ESCALANTE: Hug each other.

CHOLO *(Disbelief)*: Kimo?

(They slowly approach each other, hug and break away quickly.)

JAIME ESCALANTE: Kiss each other.

(They approach each other cautiously. Then, unexpectedly, they embrace and kiss passionately. Rocker lifts Cholo by his nalgas off the ground. They do not stop until Escalante breaks them apart.)

Are you two Tijuana putos finished? Now, let's get to work! Now I am going to teach you how to make the house special. The "Edward James Olmos" pizza! First you knead the dough. Then you pour the "Gregorio Cortez" tomato sauce . . . see how it runs . . . some pachuco pepperonis . . . olives from Miami . . . Vice. Add some "American Me" cheese. You stick it in the oven, wait till it's farmworker brown, take it out, put it in a box, get in your lowrider and deliver it to the barrio! Did you get that?

CHOLO: Man, yo, that's as easy as uno, dos, tres.

ROCKER: Easy as A, B, C.

JAIME ESCALANTE: Let's make pizza boys!

(Jackson Five's "ABC" song is heard. They all dance and mime making pizzas to the song. Cholo and Rocker exit. Escalante suddenly has a heart attack, then recovers.)

JAIME ESCALANTE: Did I get the Academy Award yet? Anyway, the pizzeria became a success. We were making ninety pizzas a day. Times seven days a week, that's—630 pizzas. Times four weeks a month, that's—2,520. Times 365 days in a year, that's—well, you get the picture. I ran out of pinche fingers. Well, the Cholo and the Rocker, they went on to become real good buddies . . . REAL, real good buddies!

The cholo went on to become a famous Republican Hispanic politician for the Southwest.

(Cholo enters dressed in a gray, conservative suit.)

CHOLO: Members of Congress, colleagues, the grand jury . . . I'm innocent. I did not launder any money. I did not take illegal campaign funds. I remained faithful to my wife. And I didn't smoke crack with that 'ho!

JAIME ESCALANTE: I should take you to Boyle Heights and have some cholos kick your ass under the freeway. The Rocker went on to become a famous brain surgeon from Malibu . . .

(Rocker enters wearing doctor's greens, gloves and a stethoscope.)

ROCKER *(Excitedly)*: Hey nurse, the dude's on the table, give me a fucking scalpel or else he's gonna die, ain't gonna be my fuckin' fault.

JAIME ESCALANTE: Well you see, gente, it just goes to show you that not all stories end happily, because that's reality, Raza—or is it comedy? But then again we're Chicanos and *we're confused and full of rage.* But you know what? Sabes que? We're working it out . . . si se puede Raza! Órale . . .

(The three strike a pachuco pose. "In the Mood" is heard again. The giant pizza slice becomes a rocket, blasts off and flies up and out of the scene.)

Epilogue

Lights up on a beach scene. Herbert, Ric and Richard enter in beachwear.

VOICEOVER: We join our heroes as they bask in the hot summer sun of success. They're on top of the theatre world, now on to conquer new horizons, the purity and truth of their art still intact. Small talk and volleyball is all that concerns them now—secure in the knowledge that they did not sell out. La Raza is behind you now . . . miles behind.

HERBERT: You know what would make me really happy, guys?

RICHARD: What's that, Fluffy?

HERBERT: If we only had our very own television sitcom!

RICHARD: What would we call it?

RIC: Culture Clash—the sitcom! Hey, it's about time.

RICHARD: Think about what you're saying, man. We'd be million-aires, we'd forget about La Raza.

RIC: Yeah, what about our stage shows, and our tours?

RICHARD: We'd compromise everything we've done.

HERBERT: Look what happened to Freddie Prinze.

RICHARD: Look what happened to Erik Estrada.

HERBERT: We'll just do PBS television.

RICHARD, RIC & HERBERT: OK. Only PBS . . . never sell out, never sell out . . .

(The guys toast each other. Suddenly, an earthquake is felt and the floor opens up, revealing a fiery hell. La Muerte comes out, luring and seducing the guys to come and follow her.)

LA MUERTE: Come on, boys! There's lots of money, fame and fortune.

(La Muerte holds up a television set.
The guys rush in. As they descend, they are heard screaming and tearing pages out of TV scripts.)

GUYS: It's hotter than hell, está caliente! Where are we?

*(The floor starts closing in on them. They have entered Sitcom Hell.
The song "Disco Inferno" is heard as they disappear into the chasm.
Blackout.)*

RADIO MAMBO

CULTURE CLASH INVADES MIAMI

Photographs by Ken Jacques

INTRODUCTION TO *RADIO MAMBO: CULTURE CLASH INVADES MIAMI*

by Herbert Siguenza

*R*adio Mambo: Culture Clash Invades Miami* marked a turning point for Culture Clash. Both thematically and stylistically, it was the most difficult work we'd ever conceived in that it challenged us on several levels: politically, artistically and personally. It was the first piece we wrote that didn't deal specifically with West Coast Latinos. In our earlier works *The Mission, A Bowl of Beings* and *Carpa Clash*, we explored extensively the Chicano identity and aesthetic. This topic will always be near and dear to us, of course, but *Radio Mambo* provided the opportunity to broaden both our own perspective and that of our audience to embrace the greater urban mix, the multicultural story now playing in every major U.S. city.

Radio Mambo is unique among our works and, perhaps, in Chicano teatro, because it has Chicano actors giving voice to the hopes and dreams of Cubans, Haitians, Bahamians, African-Americans, Jews and an array of other cultural entities, all struggling together to find identity in a relatively young American city. Our greatest challenge in creating this work was to ensure that we played these people realistically and with dignity, avoiding broad stereotypes and shallow characterizations. Ultimately, *Radio Mambo* turned out to be a wonderful journey that took us far beyond our initial expectations.

Culture Clash first came to Miami at the behest of Maria Romeu. She gave a videotape of our PBS version of *A Bowl of Beings* to Caren Rabbino and Janine Gross of the Miami Light Project. They then brought us to South Beach to perform *A Bowl of Beings*, which turned out to be a rather revolutionary event in and of itself.

Central to *A Bowl of Beings* is the sketch "The Return of Che." We had no idea how a Miami audience would react to this blatantly irreverent look at an icon of the Left. Sure enough, gasps were heard when we hoisted the giant Che Guevara banner. No local group would have been so daring, particularly given the presence of so many right-wing Cubans in the Miami area. By the end of the show, however, people were on their feet, calling for more irreverent Chicanismo. After the performance, we found that the liberal and professional second-generation Cubans, in particular, were enthusiastic about what to them was our refreshing take on Latinos living in the U.S. By the end of the evening, there was talk about bringing us back to do a piece about Miami.

Backed by a Rockefeller grant, Miami Light commissioned us to create a work about its city. Since we were outsiders, it was important for there to be a structure to facilitate our relationship with, and truthful understanding of, the community. To that end, Miami Light formed a New Works Committee, made up of twenty-three people of varying ethnic and social backgrounds, to advise us on the project. The committee drafted a list of two hundred potential interviewees, from which we chose seventy to interview over the period of a two-month residency.

At first, we were a bit apprehensive about doing a piece on Miami, especially the Cuban angle. It's no secret that there's a long-standing political animosity between Cubans and Mexicans. The substantial exiled, right-wing Cuban community is both well-organized and outspoken about all matters anti-Castro. In contrast, the Chicano movement has long been supportive of the Cuban revolution. In Miami, Chicanos/Mexican-Americans are one of the smallest and least visible of the city's Latino groups. So it was with a particular sense of irony that we, a trio of Chicano/Latinos from Los Angeles, took on the task of holding a mirror to

Miami's gloriously faceted yet fractured culture. It was time for their mango colonic.

Despite our initial preconceptions, we discovered a Cuban community with a diverse array of political ideologies. Our own views were changed, and we began to see similarities between Mexican-Americans and Cubans. Both, and indeed many immigrant groups, share the nostalgia for a lost homeland to which they can never return. Of course there were also the obvious differences: economically and politically, Cuban Miamians have an edge over California's Mexican-Americans.

We found an even stronger connection to the Haitian population. Like Mexicans and Central Americans in California, they are an unwanted, and widely unskilled, immigrant population. The Haitian has had to contend with immigration policies that generally favor the Cubans, as well as competition from African-Americans for service-sector jobs. In addition, there's a tremendous distrust between the Haitians and the African-Americans, despite their common racial ancestry.

The story of African-Americans in Miami, as in so many other American cities, is a familiar tragedy. Although they were the founders of the city, they now find themselves at the bottom of the economic ladder. With ever-encroaching mainstream development on one side, and the aggressive capitalism of the Cuban exile population on the other, the African-American has been all but squeezed out of the picture. As in L.A., once-thriving African-American neighborhoods have been physically dissected by freeways and urban renewal.

Yet there's more to Miami than these groups. There was also the phenomenon of South Beach, a surreal oasis from blight and interracial hostilities. Here, in a kind of domestic Club Med populated by beautiful models, a fabulist environment thrives on the sustenance of both legal and illicit international monopoly capital. We found a colorful array of people to interview there: young investors, hip gallery owners, expatriate New Yorker retirees, drag queens, Pulitzer Prize-winning journalists, Marielito club owners and the many others who inhabit this strange Tropicopolis.

We went out with video camera in hand and interviewed the

Miamians. Then, after transcribing and editing dozens of hours of tape, we put together our first rough script. We hired our former collaborator, José Luis Valenzuela, to direct the first version of the piece. Initially, the script included a narrative structure based on the takeover of a fictional radio station, based in part on the exile-run, ultra-conservative Radio Mambí of Miami. This is how the piece got its title. The work premiered for three performances in November of 1994, and it was a resounding success. All the different ethnic groups and communities came out to see it, albeit with added security.

We thought at first that that was the end of *Radio Mambo*. But in 1996 we were persuaded that the piece might be of interest to those outside Miami, and so we decided to restage it in our own hometown. We hired writer-performer Roger Guenveur Smith, whose own *A Huey P. Newton Story* was a work of documentary theatre, to restage the piece. His version, which was a substantial reworking of the Miami material (including the elimination of the radio-takeover construct) was a hit in L.A. and elsewhere and has gone on to become one of our greatest successes.

PRODUCTION HISTORY

Radio Mambo: Culture Clash Invades Miami received its premiere in November 1994 at the Colony Theatre in Miami Beach, Florida, under the direction of José Luis Valenzuela. This production was commissioned and produced by The Miami Light Project.

In November 1996, *Radio Mambo: Culture Clash Invades Miami* was produced at San Diego Repertory Theatre with the following cast and creative contributors:

Ensemble	Richard Montoya, Ric Salinas and Herbert Siguenza
Director	Roger Guenveur Smith
Sets	Herbert Siguenza
Costumes	Elena Prietto
Lights	Lonnie Alcaraz and Jeff Rowlings
Sound	Mark Friedman
Stage Manager	Nora Kessler
Choreography	Lettie Ibarra

Radio Mambo also had runs at the Tamarind Theatre, Los Angeles, California; INTAR Hispanic American Arts Center, New York, New York; South Coast Repertory, Costa Mesa, California and Brava Theater Center, San Francisco, California.

LIST OF SCENES

Introduction
Radio Announcement
Deep South
Notion Lady 1
Che at Starfish
Torino Furniture
Art Dealer
We Will Rebuild
Tea for Two
Charlie Cinnamon
Don Fidel
Notion Lady 2
Cuban Gothic
The Hurricane
Haitian Neighbor
Dead Men Walking
La Ambientista
Natural-Born Tree Killers
3 A.M. in Miami (Spokenworld)
Café Nostalgia
The Architect, the Shrink and the Blind Man

Place
Miami, Florida

Time
Past, Present and Future

Introduction

Miami Vice theme is heard, then the sound of a samba whistle.

Lights come up, revealing Herbert dancing the samba. He dances, he waves, he stops for a beat, then continues. He stops and addresses the audience.

HERBERT: Hi! Welcome to *Radio Mambo: Culture Clash Invades Miami.* Now you may be asking, who the hell is Culture Clash, and why are we invading Miami? Well, Culture Clash is a Chicano theatre group out of Los Angeles. *(Strikes a pachuco pose)* Órale! We were performing one of our pieces in Miami and some producers saw our work, and they loved it of course! So they commissioned us to write a play about the people and voices of Miami. What we basically did was interview dozens of Miamians, young and old, Haitians, African-Americans, Jewish people, even Mexican farmworkers in the area of Homestead, which is south of Miami . . . and as you know, Miami is a very Cuban city, which really intrigued us, because we love the Cuban culture, the food, the music. See, the Cuban revolution influenced the Chicano movement of the '60s. I had the opportunity to go to Havana in 1981 to study theatre, and I was very impressed by their high level of education . . .

(A Cuban right-wing gentleman wearing a guayabera shirt, a panama hat, and carrying a cigar enters the theatre from the audience and approaches the stage. Herbert notices him but continues.)

. . . I didn't see a society that censored its artists. I saw a society with a one hundred percent literacy rate; I saw a society with free health care, transportation, housing . . . *(To Cuban)* Excuse me, sir, I think there are some seats up there, thanks for coming . . .

(The Cuban looks around but stays put.)

. . . a just society led by a charismatic, dynamic leader.

(Another right-wing Cuban enters. Herbert is nervous but continues.)

. . . I saw a society lending a hand to the liberation struggles of Angola, Nicaragua, El Salvador . . .

(The Cuban gentlemen step onto the stage and move toward Herbert. Herbert, nervous, steps back but continues talking.)

. . . A society of teachers, intellectuals, students, um, a society building for a better tomorrow, a society of hope, um, um, a society of love. . . . Enjoy the show, folks!!!

(Herbert exits quickly. The two Cubans meet in the middle of the stage and then run after Herbert.
The sound of a radio dial is heard moving from station to station.)

Radio Announcement

VOICEOVER: W.A.I.Q . . . Aquí Radio Mambí la Grande . . .

(German is heard, then static.)

Welcome to greater Miami and the beaches. If you are departing from a car rental agency, consult your map and safety tips. Know where you are going before departing on your journey, journey, journey . . .

Deep South

Lights up on an African-American male wearing a shower cap, sunglasses and a thick, gold chain.

DEEP SOUTH: Nigger ain't got no business in Spanish Town! No, siree! They'll kill my ass for sure. You know what I'm saying? Now, when you all came to the airport and they gave you that rent-a-car map, and in the middle of the map, it had a little red square, a little red box, no names, no streets, no nothing.

Well you all can't go in there, and that's where I live. I see you on my street, and you driving a nice car. I want the car. You got on a nice suit, I want the suit. You got a Rolex on your hand, I'm gonna knock you upside your head and get what you got!

Now you tell me why I shouldn't do that? No siree, nigga ain't got no business in Spanish Town. You all ain't got no business in the red box!

Let me tell you all something. Alabama ain't the Deep South, Mississippi ain't the Deep South, Atlanta, Georgia ain't the Deep South. Miami's the Deep South! 'Cause you all can't get no motherfuckin' deeper than that! Praise Jesus, I'm telling the truth.

(Deep South flashes the letter "M" gang sign with his fingers. As Deep South exits, he bumps into the Notion Lady.)

Yo, look out bitch!

Notion Lady 1

A middle-aged, educated Cuban woman with accent.

NOTION LADY: The notion of freedom. The notion of rugged individualism is wrong. I need to be my brother's keeper. I need to know my neighbors; they need to know me. Because robbers communicate between themselves better than we do. The notion that you are at risk—a whole subculture that is living off crime, a subculture that is living off bonafide honest people. This is no longer my house. It has been raped. I'm a single woman who now lives behind bars. The notion of the haves versus the have-nots? The notion of the pursuit of materialistic wealth is the unwritten contract of Miami! *(She exits)*

Che at Starfish

Bette Midler's "Only in Miami" is heard. Che, a South Beach drag queen, storms the stage.

CHE: Hello ladies and gentlemen, and gentlemen that are drag queens! Oh, you all look fabulous tonight, or should I say flab-ulous? *(To audience member)* Because girl I have two words to say to you: Jenny Craig! Ha! I'm such a bitch. Welcome to Starfish here in Miami Beach, I'm Che. I'm from Hialeah. Hi. You know I saw Madonna here last night. Did you hear, did you hear? She got the role of Evita. It's about a prostitute who claws her way to the top. Now there's a stretch for her. Ha, I'm such a bitch! Are you all ready for the show? Where else can you get a plate of arroz con pollo served by a six-foot Cuban drag queen? Only in Miami!

(Music swells up and Che is joined by two more drag queens. The three dance, then exit.)

Torino Furniture

Mr. Torino, a Cuban merchant, enters with a chair.

TORINO: Turn that crap off! I said, turn that off. Put on the Jon Secada music. The customers like Jon Secada in the show-room, coño! So you guys want to know why Cubans are so successful? In order to understand Cubans, you have to go back in history. Basically, we were Spanish traders; Cuba was like Lebanon. Like Phoenicians, we were merchants. That's why we're aggressive, assertive, competitive. That's just our nature. I mean, that's why they call us the Jews of the Caribbean. But I say it's because of the café Cubano, the Cuban coffee!

But let's say, for example, as far as business goes, if you were to put the basic ethnics of Miami, which are your Jews, your Cubans, your American blacks, Haitians, um, Orientals. If you had them all run a hundred-yard dash, and all of a sudden, the Cuban wins. Now it doesn't make him better than the other people, but he won because of his skills, talent, drive, vigor, savvy, resilience, stamina, determination, perseverance, enthusiasm, the pep, the potency, the spirit, the verve, vitality, the energy, his cojones!

And that's what makes him better! I mean faster! And it shouldn't make the other races resentful towards him. It's survival of the fittest, man. Us Cubans, we make the opportunity, it is not given to us.

Now, I came to the U.S. in a Catholic welfare program, the Peter Pan Project, and they placed my brother and I with foster parents up in Washington State. We were like a rare species up there, being the only Cubans in captivity. See, my father who owned a furniture store back in Cuba, thought the revolution wasn't going to last. So, that's why he sent us here.

This was one of the first waves in the 1960s. We became Americanized. We struggled and worked hard, but eventually we became very successful here. In 1981 we established Tooooorinooo Furniture!! (He slams the folding chair open, revealing his company logo)

This is my store. This is my showroom. And as you can see, on this block alone I have a lot of competition, but what sets us apart has always been our tradition of advertising on TV. We like doing commercials on whatever topic is hot! For example we did one on the balseros, the rafters. We did a boat people coming from Cuba thing. And boy did it rouse the Latin community, but as long as it had them talking, it was publicity. We didn't give a shit! What we did was this. (He moves the chair downstage, using it as a boat)

We get my boat, we get a raft, we get a homemade raft and we put it out in the middle of the ocean. Then we get my brother's son and daughter, and we put them on the raft, ah, also with their collie dog, "Mambo." And, then I get on my boat with my brother, a camera, and the scene goes like this: my brother yells at them, "De donde vienen?" Where are you coming from? And they answer, "De Cuba!" From Cuba. And then he asks them, "Y adonde van?" Where are you going? "To Tooooorinooo Furniture!!!!"

So man, let me tell you, the phone, every time we aired it! Our sales went up! We even had rafters, the Marielitos, come in and tell us they didn't mind our ad, "We loved it." And at the same time we had the phone ringing, telling us, "Listen, get that goddamn ad off the air, we lost relatives and people in the rafts."

I said, "Hey listen, we aren't doing this against anyone, we're doing it because it was a hot topic and it brings us business." In fact, our next ad is gonna be about the Persian Gulf crisis! I'm going be dressed up as Saddam Hussein. I mean, he looks Hispanic, right? I'll be yelling at some G.I.s, "Yankee go home, go back, go back to America and bring me a love seat from Toooorinooo Furniture!!!!" Toorinooo Furniture! Ha, ha, ha! *(He exits)*

Art Dealer

The sound of a gentle surf crashing on a beach is heard. A hip South Beach art dealer wearing sunglasses enters. He frames the audience with his hands like a movie director.

ART DEALER: Anglos, Jews, I am a Jew, but now Jews are considered Anglo. *(Nervous laugh)* Oh, boy, I believe that in an abstract and metaphorical sense, that, South Beach should be: one third black, one third Hispanic, and one third Anglo, with each of its respective gay communities within. There is a terrible component here, *(Pointing off stage to "Overtown," the black section of Miami)* over there.

(Paco #1, the Art Dealer's assistant, enters holding an empty frame in front of his face.)

But the African influence is very alive in all the artwork that I buy and sell. This piece is entitled "Changó." *(Anglo accent)* Más arriba por favor. Gracias, Paco.

(Paco #1 exits.)

(Apologetically) You have to speak Spanish in order to conduct business here in Southern Florida. I love Spanish. I love Spain. I feel very connected to the Spanish people. Madrid, *(Castillian accent)* Bar-the-lona. I love its influence here in Miami, but of course it came to Cuba first. I mean Cooo-ba, pardon me.

Carlos Alfonzo was a terrific friend of mine, and of course the influence is very apparent in his work.

(Paco #2, another assistant, enters with an empty frame in front of his crotch.)

(Anglo accent) Más abajo por favor. Gracias Paco, en el baño, por favor. Where else would it go?

(Paco #2 exits.)

Taking the best of the old and adding the new. Bringing something bold, exciting and responsible to the mix. Embellishing the old, leaving the past to go boldly into future.

(Paco #1 and #2 enter holding a large empty frame.)

As you can see, this work is very powerful . . . *(Overly dramatic)* The vast emptiness that you feel . . . "gestalt" . . . yet . . . gracias Pacos.

(The Pacos exit.)

This is a neighborhood in transition, and as the neighborhood begins its transition, we must be careful that the people who lived here before continue to live here, the less fortunate, at least a small portion of them.

There are some very good poor people, there are some very bad poor people, crack addicts. We have an elderly Jewish population, an emerging Hispanic group, a large black population, and a throbbing, I mean thriving, gay community.

This is a great area with lots of character. It has been gentrified a lot. We have to create this kind of community, you see. The elderly population has moved away or died off and they have not been replaced yet. *(He exits)*

We Will Rebuild

Jackhammers and city sounds are heard. A city developer wearing a hardhat and carrying architectural plans enters.

DEVELOPER: International trade is becoming now the main business in Miami. Latin American companies are now moving their corporate headquarters to Miami. Before it was Havana if you wanted to conduct any type of business, but now it's Miami. There's a great future here, the weather is great, Spanish is spoken, it lends itself to a good business climate. In a certain sense you could say Miami is the capital of Latin America!

(Two construction workers wearing hardhats and carrying an I-beam enter.)

(To men) Right through there, Pacos. My firm and I work very closely with the community. I'm the chair of this group called

We Will Rebuild, which is primarily rebuilding the southland, after Hurricane Andrew. It was formed by Alva Chapman, who is what you might call our senior Anglo guru. The guy who was able to convene the right folks, if you know what I mean. All in all we raised about twenty-eight million dollars, and we distributed it to a wide variety of groups, housing groups, day care centers, whatever may be needed. Of course we didn't want to replace what was *there* because a lot of what was *there* was no good.

Sure, Miami has its share of problems just like any American city. Let's see now, we had riots in the '60s; we had riots in the '70s . . . gosh darn it, we had riots in the '80s, too! Quite recently we had the black-American-led boycott of the tourist industry. This was caused when Nelson Mandela came to this country. Apparently he told CNN news that Fidel Castro was very good to him while he was in prison . . . oh, oh, time out . . . *(Secretive)* See Fidel Castro around here is the devil incarnate. He doesn't get any credit for anything he does. So, when Mandela arrived to Miami, well, he was snubbed by some local government folks, just wasn't treated properly, given keys to the city, that type of thing. And this really angered the black community, and this triggered the boycott, preventing conventions from coming to town, tourist monies, this type of thing, really giving Miami a black eye. Ha, ha ha! *(Embarrassed)* Well, you know what I mean.

Only the city of Miami Beach, which isn't Hispanic, treated Mandela in any way; otherwise he was not treated very. . . . Oh watch out for that girder, it almost took your head off! But I really believe that the boycott was triggered by the fact that there is a tremendous economic difference between the black community and everyone else. They're just not in the same ballpark, if you know what I mean. There's a good example right there, over the river.

(Pointing) That's Overtown. Now, Overtown used to be a very vibrant community; they had black-owned nightclubs, theatres, before World War II. Then, they built the expressway, right smack in the middle of it, and the whole concept of urban

renewal cleared blocks at a time. Of course nothing ever happened. No one rebuilt. And now it's a ghost town. Come on, step this way, I'll show you some condos overlooking the ocean. I swear, on a clear day you can see Havana. *(He exits)*

Tea for Two

An old Duke Ellington song is heard. A Cuban waiter enters with two chairs and places them down, then sets an imaginary table. Two elderly black ladies enter and sit at the table. The waiter serves them tea and exits.

DOROTHY: Well, when it comes to black history in Southern Florida it has been either denied or neglected. Years ago, I went to the Miami Public Library to look for black history, and I was given a folder of obituaries. And I asked the nice lady behind the counter, "Why?" And she said to me, "Maybe those people haven't thought enough of themselves to write their own history." People in this county have amnesia.

Now, Miami was incorporated as a city in 1896. *(Kidding)* You remember, don't you? And one third of the men who stood for the corporation were black. You see, the charter needed three hundred and fifty signatures of registered voters, and at the time there were not enough white men who were registered. And back then . . . *(Secretive)* There were no Mr. Mascanosas or Mr. Gomezes, *(Referring to the waiter and the entire Latino community)* there was none of this. However, these same African-American men were not allowed to live or buy property within the city limits. And there was this god-awful curfew, which restricted black folks from being on the streets of Miami at certain times of the day. I am telling you, early Miami was a racist city in the most vicious sense of the word! I still get unladylike just thinking about it.

When Miami became a city, we became second-class citizens. When we built the railroad, we were placed adjacent to downtown. Back then they called it Colored Town, or the Central Negro District, or Overtown; that's what the people called it. And later, when white downtown wanted to expand, it couldn't go east because it would go into the bay and west was the Miami River, so they expanded right into Overtown. And they built their big old expressway which further divided the community.

And I don't think they understood what a flourishing, vibrant community it was. It was self-contained, self-operated. We were treated like first-class citizens in Overtown. No ma'am, most local history books still tend to sugarcoat the founding of Miami and the building of the railroad. Yes, indeed, I would have to say that people in this county have amnesia.

(The Cuban waiter comes back in and pours more tea.)

MARGO: That's very interesting, Dorothy, but my experience here in Miami has been totally different, coming from New York. The retirement lifestyle, living on the beach is great, but from what I see of Miami, what we call Miami, not Bell Harbor or Sunny Isles, I don't see any mixing here at all. *(She dismisses the Cuban waiter with disdain)* There are definitely divisions worse here than I have seen in a long, long time.

Way back in segregation days, what we call blacks now, they lived in one section or two sections. Now you have black Haitians living in Little Haiti, or black Cubans living in Wildwood, or some name I can't think of. And then you have people who live in, uhm, Oak . . . oh you were just talking about it.

DOROTHY: Overtown.

MARGO: Overtown! Those people don't meet other people. Now you're going to have to pardon me, Dorothy, but these are just my observations. You go into Overtown, and they look at you like you're from outer space. They just don't know any other people. And they're limited to their own environment, which is very bad, very bad. They don't even know how to dress. They have their own style, their own hairstyles. They have the gold teeth and all those things which other people just don't have. Right here in Florida, in Miami mostly, they come to work to the library, to the main library, in what I would call cocktail dresses. Something you would wear to a cocktail party. One day I was in an elevator, and a nice-looking girl walks in, nice figure and all. She had on black lace. *(Hushed tone)* This was twelve noon. That kind of thing. And then the teachers come to the library wearing halter tops, so the students copy the teacher, and they wear halter tops. So you have boys and girls, teenagers dressed like they're going to a barbecue.

There are just no standards. Danielle, my daughter, you know Danielle. She was working at a radio station in Coconut Grove, and she said that there were no dress standards there. She says that they would come in . . . *(Hushed tone)* no stockings. These were the salespeople with sandals and no stockings. And they just thought this was perfectly OK. So these are the differences we find here in Miami. There's no question the signs are down. The white and the colored fountain signs. We know that. See in New York we didn't have signs. We just knew where we couldn't go. But I was down here in Miami in 1934 dancing with Lena Horne.

DOROTHY *(Excited)*: You danced with Lena? I love Lena Horne.

MARGO: Of course I did! Lena couldn't stay at any of the hotels on the beach. And on the night she did, they burnt her bedsheets the next morning. Duke Ellington or Cab Calloway, I can't remember, they had to sneak through the back, through the kitchen. These were bandleaders, Dorothy. *(Pause)* Having come a long way, I used to say that the next generation would be different. Is it different? I don't think so. They might not call you a name, as a rule, but there's still this feeling, there's still this thinking, and it's a tradition of the family. I always thought when the younger generation came along, there would be no more problems. That everything would be fine.

(Music blasts in abruptly. Waiter comes in dancing. The ladies exit. The waiter clears the table while dancing to a medley of musical styles: Latin hip-hop, merengue, salsa, calypso, reggae, ending with West Coast Chicano music. He does a pachuco pose and exits.)

Charlie Cinnamon

We hear "Oh, Me, Oh Miami" from the movie Moon Over Miami. *A cameraman, a sound man and Charlie Cinnamon—a Jewish, South*

Beach, public-relations man—enter, miming as if in a silent movie. The cameraman and sound man chase Charlie. They all sit. The music stops.

CHARLIE: In Miami we have a bunch of yentas, you know what is the yenta? Did you see the movie *Fiddler on the Roof*? Well, in the movie *Fiddler on the Roof*, you had the yenta. She was the matchmaker, the one who brought the two young lovers together. And, there was a whole community of people and all they did was gossip, gossip, gossip, the yentas! Maybe there is a word in your language for yenta . . . ?

CAMERAMAN: Uh . . . Geraldo Rivera?

CHARLIE: Oh, Jerry Rivers, he's a Jew, you know! *(Pause)* Anyway, I came to Miami from New York, surprise! I was doing public relations in the theatre. And, I have a wonderful story that I would like to tell you, absolutely true story. When my father and my uncles came through Ellis Island, there was some confusion with the authorities. The INS people. And, they said, "What is your name?" And, my father and uncles of course didn't understand the language, scared to death. So, the authorities said "We're gonna give you a name," and as a result one uncle came out Zimmerman, one came out Timmerman, and my father came out Cinnamon! *(Referring to himself)* Charlie Cinammon. Had to be there, I suppose. We lived in the Bronx, and it was an absolutely wonderful time. Everybody got along, there was no animosity, no prejudice, your Irish kids played with your Jewish kids, the Jewish kids played with your Spanish kids, and of course your Puerto Rican kids played with your little colored kids, absolutely wonderful situation, if you ask me.

I came to Miami at a wonderful time, it was the end of the gambling era, your cloak and suit crowd straight out of New York. You had your Walter Winchells running around with Sophie Tuckers, Jimmy Durante, of course, your Ricky Ricardos and Jackie Gleasons came much later. Frankie Sinatra was runnin' around with his goon squad so it was a bit of a vulgar period, too. You know who was running around here? Did you see *The Godfather*? Who was the gangster, the little man?

SOUND MAN: Al Pacino?

CHARLIE: No, the little man, you know, the Lee Strasberg character . . . Meyer Lansky! I saw Meyer Lansky. Scared the hell outta me, I said, "Hello Meyer, good-bye Meyer." He was a killer, you know. He would walk his dog on the beach. The dog could take a shit right on your shoes. "Thanks for the shoeshine, Meyer." Back in the day we had what we called "this year's hotel"—one year it would be the Fountainebleau, the next year it would be the Casablanca. Of course, now, you see these major magnificent hotels just sort of crumbling over there on Collins Avenue.

Back in the day, some of the hotels had what they called "The Restricted Covenant." *(To cameraman)* Be sure to get this, Spike Lee, "Restricted Covenant." That means they had signs right over the main entryway, "Gentiles Only." You know what that means? Huh? No Jews! No Jews! People don't wanna talk about this, Charlie Cinnamon remembers these things.

And, if you was black, forget it. You was in the kitchen or onstage. I saw Harry Belafonte one night on the mainstage at the Copa. You remember the banana guy? *(Sings)* Day-o, Day— . . . before your time. As soon as he was done, they bussed him back to Overtown. Terrible, the goyem could be awfully funny and cruel that way. Of course, when Sammy Davis, Jr. came to town he confused the hell out of them. Is he black? Is he a Jew? Does he have one eye; does he have two? You know.

Then, the whole place sort of became this amazing shit hole, and then the Cubans came in and over time, with their ingenuity, their know-how and money, they fixed the place up. And, that has caused a lot of friction . . . *(Secretive)* between the Cubans and, uh . . . everybody else. They're very uptight people. I think it's the Cuban coffee they drink. I dunno. They had an art show at a gallery here, and a bomb went off. Huh? You gonna have extra security at your show? Maybe I might go. I dunno.

SOUND MAN: Charlie, as you know we're from L.A. Do you like L.A.?

CHARLIE: Los Angeles? *(Referring to the camera)* Is this on? Fuck L.A.! I hate L.A. Nothing but a bunch of backstabbing cock-suckers, everybody's in therapy. You don't know what your next job's gonna be. Keep your Los Angeles.

The phone is driving me crazy, you mind? *(He picks up an imaginary phone)* Charlie Cinnamon, public relations. George! You mensch. How are you? I'm sort of busy right now, you'll never believe who's in my office. No. *This Is Your Life.* They're interviewing me for a show, the Culture Club boys are here. *(Puts his hand over the phone and whispers:)* George works for *The Herald. (Back to the phone)* They're gonna put my story up on the stage, imagine. I think the bald one is gonna do me. *(Pause)* He's gonna play me, you sick bastard! I'm gonna come over there and stab you in the eyeball. Call me back, sure. What? Spalding Gray is coming to town. I did not know that. With a new show? A new chair, a new table? We gotta see this, George. Call me later. We'll do dinner. Good-bye. *(He slams the phone down)*

Shmuck! Where were we?

SOUND MAN: The Cubans.

CHARLIE: Oh, yeah. Well, this might not be a politically polite thing to say, but it's my business, but there is a cultural difference that centers around the language. I'll give you a perfect example. The other day I'm standing in an elevator downtown. The doors open wide. A nice young Cuban couple gets on the elevator, very sophisticated, very good-looking, like yourselves . . . not. So, I'm standing there and they start speaking in Cuban.

SOUND MAN: Spanish.

CHARLIE: Yeah, the Cuban. And, I'm thinking this is very rude. Hello, I'm standing here. If I was here with my Jewish friends, I would not speak Yiddish in front of you if I knew you did not speak the language. You love your culture. I love my culture, but you have to learn the language. That's what my father and my uncles said when they came in through Ellis Island, "You have to learn the language in order to make your way into the new world." They said it in Yiddish, but they said it, nevertheless. And, don't forget boys, "English Only" got its start right here in Southern Florida. So, these kids are yapping away there, and I'm getting a little pissed off, but the thing I cannot understand, the thing that scares the hell out of me is how fast they talk! *(Long pause)*

So, who you fellas interviewing next?

SOUND MAN *(Rapid Cuban Spanish)*: Bueno. Vamos a entrevistar unos Cubanos en la Calle Ocho.

CAMERAMAN *(Rapid Cuban Spanish)*: Vamos al restaurante, "Versailles," con la musica de Albita . . .

CHARLIE: Oy vey!

Don Fidel

Richard, Ric and Herbert transform into a singing Cuban combo standing on a street corner. Herbert keeps the beat with a clave. They sing:

Cuando Fidel murió en su cama Caribeña
Todo el mundo esta cantando, Calle Ocho esta bailando
Cuando Fidel murió en su cama Caribeña
When Fidel dies in his Caribbean bed
Todo el mundo esta cantando
All the world is singing
Calle Ocho esta bailando
Eight Street will be dancing

Don Fidel, Don Fidel, Don Fidel

Múevete Comunista
Aquí viene South Beach
Move over Comunista
Here comes Armani Exchange
Múevete Comunista
Aquí viene Gloria Estefan
Move over Comunista
Aquí viene Windows 95
Múevete Comunista
Aquí viene
El Pope John Paul
Múevete Comunista
Aquí viene Starbucks Coffee
Move over Comunista
Aquí viene Daisy Fuentes
Múevete Comunista
Aquí viene Pat Buchanan

Uy! Todo el mundo está cantando, Calle Ocho está bailando
Don Fidél!

Viva Andy Garcia, fuckers!

(Alarm sounds explode. They all exit.
    The Notion Lady reenters. She turns off the home alarm and
sits down.)

Notion Lady 2

NOTION LADY: The notion that there is total impunity. The notion that there is total disregard for human life. These folks have no understanding of the value of human life, theirs, or anybody else's. It's where it begins. It's very frightening. The notion that we are living in a jungle, in Miami.

(During the following speech, a man pointing a gun enters. He circles behind Notion Lady and exits.)

I was almost killed out of stupidity. I had a .45 against my head. He was so nervous he could've killed me without meaning to! They thought I had drugs. *(Indignant)* "How dare you confuse me!" *(Pause)* There were four of them, young, Latino, gorgeous. . . . I tried to go for my gun, and he caught me. I went for my .38. It was loaded. I would have shot the bastards! The notion that I would've been capable. . . . Some people just think about it. I had the opportunity.

The notion that I would've done that, has done something to my inner psyche that has been more detrimental, more mind-boggling, than whatever they took. Whatever they took is irrelevant. I came to this country with three dresses. So as long as I have more than three dresses, I'm ahead of the game! I'm not here to accumulate shit!

(Notion Lady exits. Blackout.)

Cuban Gothic

Celia Cruz' "Cuando Salí De Cuba" is heard.

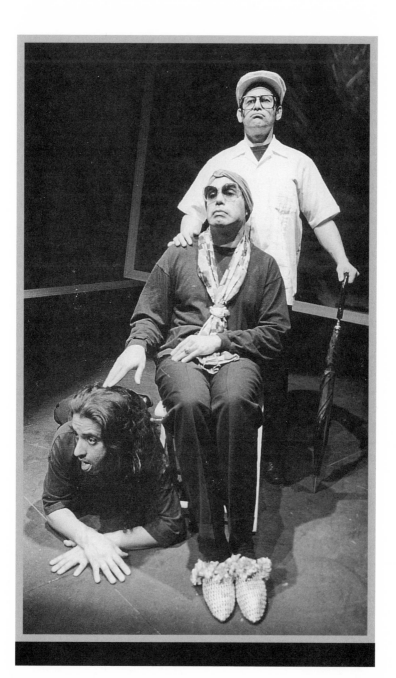

Lights fade up slowly, revealing Mr. and Mrs. Romero and an actor playing a dog. The Romeros are a conservative, upper-middle-class Cuban couple.

MRS. ROMERO: Realmente me cuesta hablar. Realmente fue muy duro. Nosotros estabamos bien plantados en Cuba, eramos de clase media, no queriamos ni visitar Miami. No. Salimos de Cuba en 1960.

MR. ROMERO *(Translating)*: We left Cuba in 1960.

MRS. ROMERO: Quisas nos asustamos. El gobrierno se estaba metiendo en los textos que estaban estudiando los muchachos en el colegio católico. Dejamos todo atrás por nuestros principios, por nuestra religión, por los dos niños que tenemos, dejamos todo atrás.

MR. ROMERO: We left everything.

MRS. ROMERO: Eso fue una cosa terrible. *(Upset)* Que lo desprenden uno de su casa, sabe?

(The dog yelps and is comforted by Mrs. Romero. Mr. Romero comforts Mrs. Romero.)

MRS. ROMERO: Salí con seis maletas, nada mas. Yo le pregunto a mi hijito, "Que es lo que tu quieres llevar?" "Mis libros, Mama, mis libritos. Eso es lo que yo quiero llevar." Yo no puedo perdonarlo. Yo he tratado y no he podido. Yo ni le digo su nombre a ese señor.

MR. ROMERO: She never says his name.

MRS. ROMERO: El sacerdote me dice que hay que rezar por el. Si le digo, yo rezo, pero yo rezo para que ese come mierda se vaya al cielo!

(Mrs. Romero starts weeping and continues to comfort the dog. Mr. Romero comforts his wife and continues the interview.)

MR. ROMERO: Nosotros perteneciamos a un grupo muy privilegiado. We were the privileged ones. Acostumbrados a una vida elitista! We put Fidel in power. At the time Cuba had Batista, un mulatto. Fidel era un muchacho carismatico, educated, Jesuita. This one is one of us, we say. Good family, alto, gallego, blanco. Fidel was the only one that say no to the United States. The rest of Latin America say bravo, Fidel, bravo! But the ones who suffered, the ones who pay the price, were the Cubans. We had high hopes for the revolucion. Lo terrible fue la traición. Engaño al pueblo. He tricked us!

(Mournfully) My primo, a med student, was given fifteen years for passing out flyers, fifteen years! My uncle was waken up and taken out in the middle of the night, we never heard from him again. Esa es la realidad Cubana!

Sometimes I wonder what would happen if we would have stayed. We left thinking we were going to come back soon, that the revolution wasn't going to last. Maybe it was out of fear, or that we were selfish. But we abandoned our country, we abandoned our country. Maybe he would have changed. He couldn't kill us all; he couldn't incarcerate 900,000 of us. We had the option to stay. We were the middle class, the educated, the thinkers, los inteligentes. Fidel wasn't going to last. How could he? The ones that stayed behind were the poor, los guajiros, los brutos . . . los negros. But once again, he tricked us, because he educated them, he trained them, and thirty-nine years later here we are still waiting.

(The sound of a storm is heard. The Romeros stand and cover themselves with an umbrella, forming a tableau. The dog begins to bark wildly.)

MRS. ROMERO: Mambo! Ven pá, ca Mambo, Mambo!

(The Romeros exit. The dog begins to chase its tail. As it does so, it becomes more human, crouching down on all fours. The storm grows into a hurricane. The human figure becomes a hurricane victim hiding for cover, using only a flashlight to light her face.)

The Hurricane

LILIBETH *(Hushed tone)*: It was dark. And the dark is very frightening you know. But I remember most of all the sound, the
noise; it was like a thousand lions roaring at the same time.
My god it was frightening. And in this house twenty trunks of
whole trees fell this way, and you know what we heard of the
trees? *(Snapping fingers)* Tic, tic, tic . . . That little noise was
loud enough to wake up every animal in the jungle, but it was
the sound of the lion roaring; my god, you drowned in your
fear.

And if that was not enough, you hear the choo-choo train
coming, chick-a-chick-a-chick, and you know when you hear
the choo-choo train coming, it is the storm, the tornado, digo
the hurricane. And of course this is all happening at three
o'clock in the morning and it continues until four o'clock, five
o'clock, six o'clock, finally at seven in the morning it begins to
die down, and you go outside to take a look, and my god, you
are not prepared for what you are about to see.

Blue sky. Nothing but a sea of blue; you have never seen so
much blue sky in Miami. Where is everything; where's the
trees and the houses?

You are not prepared for such complete and utter, indis-
criminate devastation. And then it hits you. Mother Nature,
she is so powerful. What are you going to do with a force so
powerful? I tell you what you are going to do, you are going
to huddle up with your familia like little animals and pray to
your god above, whoever she is.

And in these moments you begin to clutch and grab for
your prized possessions. Forget about your jewelry and your
furs, I only had time to grab a small photograph of my son who
was dying of AIDS at the time he was in the hospice.

And in this house when the storm was raging, I could hear
the sound of a woman crying; it was a Seminole Indian
woman, I believe, and she cry for the loss of something, the

Everglades, her children, la tierra, it is the very Cry of Florida itself. I don't know . . . forgive me, I'm starting to sound a little like Shirley MacLaine. Let me see. In Los Angeles you have your earthquakes, yes a couple of seconds this way, a couple of seconds that way, you are in shock, but basically it's over.

In a hurricane, mijo, you wait and you wait and I tell you this, there is no electricity, no telephones, no television, no nothing. Your only connection to the outside world is your transistor radio.

(Lilibeth turns off flashlight. Blackout. Radio dial moving from station to station is heard.)

Haitian Neighbor

Lights up on the Haitian Neighbor, Viter, a distinguished, middle-aged community activist.

VITER: Aye Vincent! Change the station, change the station. Put on the Haitian music, s'il vous plait.

(Radio dial turns and stops on "Me So Horny" by 2 Live Crew.)

I say Haitian music!

(Music finally changes to Haitian music.)

That's not funny! Ha, ha, ha. My son Vincent. Ooh it's hot. Ooh. Hot. Do you want drink? A rum and coke? I'll have drink for you. I had long day at community center.

Do I love Miami? Yes I say, because yes more than any other place in the United States, Miami, I love it. Why? Because I use to say, Miami, in many aspects is like Haiti, without the poverty.

So, I do love Miami. I love Miamians. I never suffered from so-called segregation, because I stay in my territory, I know my limits. And I won't allow anyone to cross over in my territory and play game, no! I will protect myself to the full extent. But also, I know where my right starts and my duty starts. I can look over, and see the grass might be greener on my neighbor's yard, but it's his grass. I have grass. You enjoy yours, I enjoy mine; we remain good neighbors, that's Miami.

(Vincent crosses past his father. He is dressed in hip-hop fashion: Miami baseball cap and jersey and a thick gold chain.)

VINCENT: Yo, what's up, Pops?

VITER: Vincent, say hello to the people from California.

VINCENT *(Indifferent)*: What's up? Yo, Pop, I got some extra tickets to the Heat game, want to come?

VITER: No, merci. I have a board meeting at the community center tonight.

VINCENT: OK, Pops, I'll catch you later.

(Vincent tries to exit but realizes he did not kiss his father good-bye. Reluctantly, Vincent goes back to kiss Viter on one cheek. Vincent pauses and realizes he has to kiss Viter's other cheek. Embarrassed, Vincent does so and exits.)

VITER: Au revoir! Bon chance!

VINCENT: Speak English, pops. English. And turn off this damn jungle music. It's embarrassing.

VITER: Ha, ha, ha, my son Vincent. He likes Snoop Doggy Doggy. I always say, American people are as good as any people in the world. American system is something else. When I was in New York City, I was lost in the subway. My English was worst than it is now. I was looking around. One white guy say to me, "Hey can I help you?" "I want to go to downtown," I said. There was no way to cross over from uptown train to downtown train. So in cold weather, he cross the street with me. Puts ten cent, waited for me to catch downtown train. This was one white guy! So people are not the enemy. Government are the enemy and make the people pay for it. If people were enemies, French would never talk to the Germans.

I have some Cuban friends, and they always complaining about Castro. "Castro is a Communist. Castro this, Castro that." I say to them, I would prefer twenty times Castro in Haiti, than one Duvalier! Ooh, ohh! Don't say that! You and I are both sick. You have diabetes, and I have high blood pressure. As diabetic, you can take salt. As high blood pressure, I can take sugar. You can take salt, I can take sugar. We have the same kind of disease or epidemic, only different. So I say to them, you complain about Castro? I give you one Duvalier.

At least there is no Cuban who come to this country illiterate, without a skill. And the only reason they let the Cuban in, is because he can contribute to the establishment of the United States. We are talking about society, economy, not opinion. Every Haitian who come to this country, bring with him the problem created in Haiti by American policy. You are part of the problem. You must be part of the solution.

(Viter exits. Stevie Wonder's "Living for the City" is heard.)

Dead Men Walking

Three African-American inmates enter and form a jail lineup. They turn left, right and center.

CON #1: I'm twenty-eight years old. I've been in and out of the Dade County jail system half of my life. Half the people I knows, I've known in the system. The system is all I know. See, being in jail ain't the hard part; being on the street is. Know what I'm saying? I can talks about changing, but it ain't easy. There's no jobs. I got no skills. So I gots to start from scratch. I can flip burgers for three-fifty an hour or I can make three "g"s popping you upside your head and getting what you got. It's what you're down for. I'm down for the life; I'm down for the negative. I've been doing wrong for so long, that for me, doing right is wrong. I see motherfuckers in Coral Gables, Key Biscayne, big-ass homes, big-ass cars, jet skis, chauffeurs. I crave for that shit too, and I'm gonna get it by any means necessary!

CON #2: Let me elaborate on what the brother said. We're not trying to live, we're trying to survive. I can work minimum wage, but that's hardly surviving. And if I can't find a job, and I come home one day, I find my old lady's with another man.

I go, oh, oh, oh, oh. Now I'm not going to go O.J. on her, but I might get back on the dope. And I'm going to have to steal or kill for the dope. See, I take, but I've been took. I've been to jail forty times, prison twice. If I'm out on the street, a policeman can pick me up, take me in, and lock me up, and I might not be doing nothing. That's cuz I'm labeled as an H.O. Habitual Offender. An H.O. Career criminal. I'm down for the count. And if I see a tourist in my neighborhood, I want what they got, and I'll get it. I got no reason to be good.

CON #3: It's the system that gives us our attitude. Here in Miami Dade lockup, when they bring in the white boys, they book 'em in and they book 'em out. Same with the Cubanos, they in and they out of there. Then they bring in the Haitians, and sometimes they stick us in the same cell, I guess they figure black, black it's the same. No, man, it ain't the same. Them Haitians is trash, trash, low man on the totem pole. They motherfuckuhs don't even speak English! They gots to work their way to the top.

And Miami basically is the same way. I walk in to a liquor store, that Korean mothufuckuh gonna be axing me can I help you this, can I help you that, I say why? I know why. I go to a gas station, the bitch gonna be looking at my gas card up and down, all around, why? Texaco motherfuckuh. If there is a pot-hole on my street, and the rain fill that hole up with water, the water gonna stay in the hole till the sun dry it up. I pay taxes, my mamma pay taxes, too.

So when we say the system, we mean the system is what give us our attitude. One tourist, one tourist gets killed, you all gonna read about it front page news, CNN headlines. Well, niggas get killed everyday, right here, you don't read about that do ya? So what the brothers are saying is that Miami need a change, Miami need a three-hundred-and-sixty-degree change with a motherfuckin' face lift. Word.

(The three cons exit. The sound of jail doors slamming is heard. Then, a voiceover repeats: "Dead man walking. Dead man walking . . ." Then, the chirping of birds is heard.)

La Ambientista

A wealthy environmentalist wearing a sun hat and garden gloves enters.
She is holding a plant.

LA AMBIENTISTA: What do I think of Miami? Miami is a third-world
country with first-world amenities. So if you extend that, and
I do, then it's got third-world-country problems, too. For
instance, did you know that there is not a word in the Spanish
language for environment? The closest thing they have, I
believe, is ambiente. What does this mean? Ambience, atmosphere. I suppose that makes me an ambientista. *(Raising her
fist in a mock power
salute)* This just gives
me the willy-jillys.

We have lots of
environmental concerns
right here in Southern
Florida. We've got toxic
pesticides, and it's
because of the climate
everything grows, thank
you very much. So in
order to control it, we
have to use lots of pes-
ticides. We've got
phosphate mining, the
Everglades are in dan-
ger as well. They are
draining the Everglades
and the wetlands every
day in order to create
more land for agricul-
ture but primarily to
protect land for devel-

opment. And of course the powerful sugar lobby has got Mr. Clinton by the good old scrotum. A bunch of powerful Cubanos, sleeping in the Lincoln bedroom, you know. I've got two lawsuits pending there, so I can't say another word about it. El Zippo la Boca.

We've got an incinerator burning out of compliance, of course it's in the "black section" of town. You can see the smokestacks, right through the palm trees there. They look like big old Cuban cigars. And they just bellow toxic smoke, twenty-four/seven. And either the poor people of that community continue to pay for that incinerator, because they're going to pay for it with their taxes anyway. I.e.: they are going to pay if they use it, and they are going to pay if they don't. And they're going to pay the ultimate price, too. *(Coughs)* I think you know what I mean. This sort of situation promotes generations of trash, and it promotes more usage of illegal incinerators. It just gives me the willy-jillys.

(Pacos #1 and #2 enter, each holding empty art frames.)

Hola. Oh, my goodness, I have been waiting for these forever! They're stunning. Could you please put those in the pool house?

(They do not understand.)

La casa de la pool. Gracias.

(Pacos #1 and #2 exit.)

Warhols. Originals. It's the Jew series. You saw there, ah, Gertrude Stein, Bertolt Brecht, Groucho Marx, Karl Marx, Louis Farrakhan. . . . That's a joke! Come on. You got kind of quiet on me. The funny thing is, Louis Farrakhan is probably more of a Jew than I am. I mean don't get me wrong, I had both of my boys circumcised and everything, but you will never catch me on the front lines of the JDL. I mean religion, please, I've had it up to here with religion. But if you cut down a tree, I will hunt you down and I will kill you!

(Sounds from the chainsaw scene in the movie Scarface *are heard. La Ambientista grabs her plant and exits.)*

Natural-Born Tree Killers

Francis is performing fellatio on her husband, Todd, while he watches Scarface *on TV. She is a second-generation Cuban-American. He is a blue-collar Anglo.*

TODD: Ah, that's good baby, yeah, mmmm. Hey honey, I love this movie, *Scarface*. Al Pacino looks just like a Cuban. Look it, this is my favorite part, when they saw the guy apart!

FRANCIS *(Looking up)*: Ooh, that's gross!

(Francis resumes performing fellatio. Suddenly, Richard's voice is heard offstage.)

RICHARD: Hello! Anybody home? Hello?

FRANCIS: It's the guys from California! It's the interview. I forgot all about it!

TODD *(Yelling)*: Shit. I'll clean up. *(To Richard)* Ah, down here, in the den. We're down here!

(Francis rushes out and Todd greets Richard.)

RICHARD: The door was open, so I just came in.

TODD: Oh, that's cool. You're the guy from California. You're Herbert?

RICHARD: No, I'm Richard.

TODD: Cool, I'm Todd.

RICHARD: Will your wife, Francis, be joining us?

TODD: Oh, yeah. *(Yelling)* Hey Francis! Francis! The guy from California is here! Don't keep him waiting, baby.

(Gargling sounds are heard offstage.)

FRANCIS: I'll be right out!

RICHARD: Is she OK? I'll come back another day.

TODD: No, she's fine. She's just flossing. We just had dinner.

(Francis comes out and greets Richard.)

FRANCIS: Hi, good to meet you. Ah, please have a seat.

(Francis and Todd sit on chairs and Richard sits on the floor. The couple's dialogue overlaps throughout.)

This is so exciting. I read about this project, but I never thought we'd be chosen.

TODD: Wow, I never met an actor from California before, this is cool. All right. We saw you in *Encino Man*.

RICHARD *(Embarrassed)*: Thank you. I hope you don't mind, I'm going to record the interview. We'll start with your names. Todd, you go first.

TODD: My name is Todd.

FRANCIS: I'm Francis. Um, Francis with an "i."

RICHARD: I understand you guys own a demolition company.

FRANCIS: Yeah, it's really my mom's. I mean you should see her at work. She tells these big machines to bulldoze this, and knock this down. She's a hard worker.

TODD: She's this little short thing. And she runs this multimillion dollar company. It's wild, she's this little Cuban lady with a hard hat, yelling, "Allá! Allá!" It's wild. She rocks.

FRANCIS: Yeah, it's really cool.

RICHARD: Hurricane Andrew. Was that big business for you?

FRANCIS: Oh, yeah, three years later and we're still doing contracts from that.

TODD: Oh, yeah, especially Homestead. The Mexicans got devastated. Roofs were off, trees were down. In fact, those trees you saw when you drove in? I replanted those from Homestead.

FRANCIS: Sometimes you can't save them, you got to cut them down, that's what we do. But it was horrible, what happened was this, there was no electricity for weeks. So we had to work out of my mom's house. And we had all my cousins working, because the phones were ringing off the hook.

TODD: Yeah, a bunch of Cubans with cellulars!

FRANCIS: Remember we had an ice chest, with beer and Cuban sandwiches? And then you would go out to the sites and couldn't find anything!

TODD: And you know why? Because all the signs, all the street signs were blown down by the winds. So you're driving along, looking for, let's say 243 Main Street. And then you go, "Where the hell is Main Street?" You couldn't find any street! It was weird.

FRANCIS: The hurricane knocked down all the addresses, signs, you couldn't find anything. Roofs were blown, cars overturned, children missing. The humidity was so bad, it made your eyes pop out. It was horrible. But it was great business for us. Out with the old and in with the new.

TODD: That's like our motto.

RICHARD: What's a typical day like for two natural-born tree killers?

TODD: Well it's easy for her. I do a lot of other stuff. I have a video company.

RICHARD: Oh, like showbiz.

TODD: No, I do weddings, funerals, quinceañeras, accidents. I like accidents.

FRANCIS: Well, we have to hit the snooze button at least six times before we ever get up. But, eventually we go to the office. City negotiations, city contracts, you know that type of thing.

TODD: Tell him about the Chinese guys.

FRANCIS: Oh yeah, there's these Chinese guys who want to develop downtown. They want to build a Chinatown, like they do in Chicago, and they have one in L.A., right?

TODD: These Chinese have millions of dollars in the bank. And they're trying to develop downtown, make it better. Because downtown is a shit hole, there's prostitutes, homeless, drug dealers, Brazilians. But they're getting resistance from the historical preservation people.

FRANCIS: Yeah they're giving these poor Chinese people a hard time. For example, there's this bell tower that they want to save, so we have to compromise and reach a happy medium and demolish around it. And these environmentalists, they have their nine-to-five jobs, they live in nice homes by the beach, high-rise condos.

TODD: I replanted some trees for some lady. In her pool house, she had original Andy War-hills. They're expensive.

So, anyway, the Chinese people are saying, Time out, time out. In China we have walls that are like, what? A thousand years old?

FRANCIS: A hundred thousand years old!

TODD: Yeah, hundred thousand years old, and you want to save this little bell tower built in the 1920s? They're getting frustrated, they're saying, *(Stereotypical Chinese accent)* Fuck it man, let's get out of here!

(Francis elbows Todd.)

What Francis?

(Pause.)

FRANCIS: Don't swear.
TODD: Oh, I'm sorry, man, I forgot you were recording.
RICHARD: It's all right, Todd, I promise we won't use *any of this.* Where does all the demolition go?
TODD: Oh, uh, landfill.
FRANCIS: And also the Everglades.
RICHARD: Is that safe?
TODD: Sure, where else are you going to put it? See the Everglades are going to last forever. That's why they call it "the Everglades." Ha, ha, ha.
FRANCIS: Oh, they found a dead body there the other day.
TODD: No shit, really? You think there'll be footage on Channel 11 tonight? I'd like to record it.
FRANCIS: Probably on *Hard Copy.* Oh, he loves *Hard Copy.* He watches it all the time!
TODD: No, I don't, Francis.

(Todd pinches Francis. Todd angrily looks away. Francis mouths "He loves it" to Richard.)

RICHARD: Do your families get along?
TODD: Don't go there, don't go there!
FRANCIS: At first my mom couldn't even look at him.
TODD: The Cuban culture is all wound up around the family. Centered around her mom. Six A.M. in the morning, the phone rings, I know who it is . . . *(Mimes handing Francis the phone)*
FRANCIS: . . . Hi, Mom.

TODD: It's her mom! And if she doesn't call back in two hours, her mom calls back saying, (Accent) Why didn't you call me, porque, porque?

FRANCIS: I haven't talked to her in a couple hours. I think I'm going to call her.

TODD: See that! I'll go weeks without talking to my folks. . . . I'm Norwegian.

RICHARD: Do you like Miami?

TODD: Oh yeah, it's great. The weather's great. Good for business. The Dolphins are playing great. I like it here.

FRANCIS: Oh, I love Miami. I mean the weather, the crime thing you really don't see it, only on the news. It's a great place for opportunity.

TODD: Maybe later, when we're older, we'll retire in the Jupiter area. But, while we're still young and aggressive, we like it right here! Right babe? (Kisses her) Isn't she cute? I love these Cubanas. (Gestures the size of her butt) Bam! You know what I mean. Bam!

(A long uncomfortable pause.)

RICHARD: OK, I'm out of here. Thank you for the interview.

TODD: That's it! Oh, that was great.

FRANCIS: Hope you got everything you needed.

TODD: You're welcome to stay, have a beer and watch *Scarface*.

RICHARD: No thanks, I have to go to a cafe and perform at a spoken-word thing, and then I'm going to a chupacabra Tupperware party. Bye! (He exits)

FRANCIS: He's kinda cute.

TODD: I bet he's a faggot. All those guys from L.A. are fags. Now, back to my movie, *Scarface*. I love this part.

(Todd turns on the TV and reenacts the Scarface chainsaw scene. Cool jazz music of Max Roach is heard.)

3 A.M. in Miami (Spokenworld)

Richard performs the following spoken-word piece with music underscore.

It's 3 A.M. in Miami
It's 3 A.M. in Miami
It's 3 A.M. in Havana
It's midnight in L.A.

LAX to Miami International
y los perros buscando caína
en mi bolsa
because it's 3 A.M. in Miami and there
is nothing on the radio.

It's 3 A.M. and I am walking the streets of a lonely
tropical storm and I am thinking primarily of Aztlán,
which of course means nothing here, just another
homeland which cannot be claimed.

Miami, how I love you
from Coral Gables to Key Biscayne
Before the gangsters
Before cocaine

Miami the fun state
the sun state
the gun state
the black-man-on-the-run state
the pardon-my-pun state
the marijuana-by-the-ton state
the can't-get-me-none state
the golden-bun state
the state the state the state that is.

The east the north the south not west
No not west at all

Wonderful fucked-up Miami
tangled up in hues of aqua green and blue
set against the backdrop of gunmetal black skin.

Chalk outlines pointing over there.
Compton to Miami
fly over space
you know what I mean.

It's 3 A.M. and I am thinking of Tonantzín,
I saw her in a Cuban magazine

I talked with Juana La Cubana
and I axed her do she wanna
smoke some marijuana
maybe mañana
under the cabana.
She looked like Lola Folana
Black like a Dominicana

Miami Dade of my counties
Tropic Cancer spreading

Beautiful mulattas stroll by casual and bored
in cat-like motions
a pair of pink flamingos pokes out my blue eye
it heals quickly
I gather myself in quick repose.

Bob Marley died right here
find the Seminole tribal chiefs
who gathered in ceremony for him.

Zora Neale Hurston fluffed and folded sheets
out at the beach.
The same sheets that covered
Southern Man, don't you understand
Is this love? Is this love? Is this love?

Miami the best of you
the blackest of you
may be gone
erased like the barrios
of California.

Let's all step back a bit
Welcome to the Zebra Lounge in O town
or Georgettes in Liberty City and the Knight Beat Club
at the Sir John Hotel.

Ladies and gentlemen please welcome Miss Billie Holiday.
Josephine Baker gonna be right next door.
Perez Prado gonna get down with Dizzy tonight, don't you know!
my goodness here comes Mr. Duke Ellington.
Oh my, it's Mr. Cab Calloway.
Mr. Calloway can I have your autograph sir?
My god, my country bumpkin Zoot Suit melts right to the
     ground.

Black and brown pachuco ghost lay alongside each other in
     cryptic vaults
containing various hipsters
hip-hopping along to a boogie-woogie death march

Miami you are black and don't I know it,
I'm a little scared but mustn't show it
just bust my rhyme like a Nuyorican poet
and with these words we'll slay all the dons
like Pacino's Michael Corleone

And no longer will your
paradigm of paradise parallel the paradox
that stalks the streets of Southern Florida.
We're talking about law and order, Amerika's Most Wanted
if you have it you must flaunt it.
Take back Amerika
clean up Amerika
we'll start in Southern Dade County and Southern Riverside
    county,
so no matter if you're a cruel Dade County cop or a Riverside
    county sheriff
the idea is to beat those spics down, contain the Negro
    Problem

Up against the wall motherfucker
oh yes, my favorite Miami position
Miami position #1

(Richard goes down on knees with hands behind his head.)

Oh yes, even from here I
can feel the long
arm of California governor
Pete "Puto" Wilson

Bad boy, bad boy,
what you gonna do?
A million Cubanos
in New Jersey.
The line gets a
little blurry.

Miami, your Fountain of Youth is a toxic cesspool
Your techno club scene sucks, but swallows.

A Chicano in Miami makes no sense at all
L.A. malathion never smelled so good.

OK.
Flash: 1959
Cuban blood flows like wine
Overtown Heroin trade to partially finance
"OPERATION BAY OF PIGS."
CIA-owned poppy fields in Mexico in full bloom.
Director Hoover cosigns the whole deal
Giancana, Traficante, Marcello
funnel millions of Chi-Mob dollars
through the keys and directly to Batista
and just to hedge their bets
another couple million to Castro
Casino protection
the Kennedy Election
a botched amphibious assault
with Negro Town dinero
I miss the voice of Miguel Piñero!

C.C.
No no! Si! Si!
CUBAN COMMUNITY
CATACLYSMIC CONCLUSION
CHRISTOPHER COLUMBUS
CATHOLIC CHURCH
CHEECH AND CHONG
CULTURAL COLONIALISM
CHRISTIAN CRUSADE
CORRUPT CONTRACT
CONTAIN CUBA
CHOCOLATE CITY
COLORED CHILDREN
CRUEL COPS
CRASHING CESSNA
CIVILIAN CESSNA
CASTRO'S CUBA
CHE'S CUBA

CIA CONSPIRACY
C.O.I.N.T.E.L.P.R.O. CONNECTION
COMMIE CHASER
COMMIE COCKSUCKER
CORPORATE COCKSUCKER
COCKSUCKING CHAMPIONSHIP
CONNIE CHUNG
KENNEDY KIDS
CROSS-CHECKING
CULTURAL CZARS
CHUPA CABRA
COINTELPRO/CLASSIFIED
COLLISION COURSE
CANE CROPS
CAREER CRIMINAL
CÉSAR CHÁVEZ
CHARLIE CINAMMON
CHARLIE CHAPLIN
CHANGE COURSE
CHRISTIAN COALITION
CORRUPT CONGRESS
CONSERVATIVE CUBANOS
CALCIFIED CUBANOS
CARIBEÑA CARIBEÑO
CONNECTIONS CONNECTIONS
CHINO CUBANA
CASATE CONMIGO
CHANGE CHONIES
CHICANO CLOWN
CLINTON'S CONFUSION
CONCERNING CUBA!
CIAO, COMPADRES!
CIAO, CUBA!

Revolucíon Compadres! Gracias. *(Waiting for response from audience. After there's no response:)* That's what I thought. Viva Fidel.
Gracias.

Café Nostalgia

Liz, a second-generation Cuban-American, and Omar, a Marielito with a heavy accent, sit at a café. They are smoking and drinking Cuban coffee.

LIZ: That's pretty good, for a Chicano.

OMAR: Que es un Chicano?

LIZ: A Chicano is like, a Cuban-American—with no money.

OMAR: Like I was saying, when I came on Mariel, I landed in Key West, and then they took us to Fort Smith, Arkansas. It was very sad, many of us were injured, sick, been hospitalized, prisoners, locos. It was very strange. We ate food from cans. When we landed it was dark, and a light drizzle was falling.

When the airplane door open, there to greet us was the Klu Klux Klan. Welcome to the United States, they say. It was very strange.

LIZ: Oh my god. Sounds like a nightmare. I didn't know you suffered like that. Anyway, Mariel changed the city for the better. And now Miami is like a blank canvas, ready for us Cuban-Americans to paint it. It's so exciting!

OMAR: We did bring a change. Pero el ballet, la opera, el cine, eso no tiene Miami ahora. Y eso fue un buen aspecto de Castro, porque nos educó y nos dio cultura. Aquí en Miami uno-se-tiene que adaptar, no como nuestros padres que decidieron quedarse Cubanos y Cubanos se quedaron. Nosotros los jóvenes podemos nadar en el agua que nos pongan.

LIZ: You are so right; we are very different from our parents. But I always wondered, what would have happened if my parents would have stayed in Cuba. At least I would have grown up in my own country. Only in Miami do I feel Cuban! And I resent that, I blame Castro for separating us . . . depriving me!

OMAR: Why don't you go see Cuba for yourself, chica? Take an airplane there tomorrow.

LIZ: I'm not going there as long as Fidel is still there!

OMAR: Fidel is not the only problem.

LIZ: He is the problem! That's why I support the embargo! And the Jesse Helms bill.

OMAR: Ave Maria, so my abuelito who is sick back in Cuba has to suffer? Why does my abuelo have to suffer because of this embargo?

LIZ: Because of Fidel, Fidel!

OMAR: Coño, there you go with Fidel again.

LIZ: Fidel made choices, se fue con los Rusos, and now he's paying the consequences. Yo lo siento por tu abuelito!

OMAR: Fidel is not paying, the Cubans are paying, mi abuelito is paying! The embargo helps Fidel. He can always blame the United States, el enemigo, los imperialistas! If you take away the embargo from Fidel, no tiene nada, he has nothing.

LIZ: You see, he wins either way. That's why I hate him. I hate communism. Eeeuu! No toilet paper, I mean really!

OMAR: Ave Maria (Pause) Sabe lo que pasa. Fidel, ya no es comunista.

LIZ: Oh, he's not a Communist? Then what is he?

OMAR: Lo que pasa es que Fidel, es un Fidelista!

LIZ: Fidelista? You're right! That's so clever! He's an egomaniac. Esta loco el señor. What sign is he anyway? I bet you he's a Leo.

OMAR: We give him supernatural powers. He's only human. We are so obsessed with Fidel.

LIZ: You're right, all we do is sit around talking about Fidel. We sound like our parents, how gross. Let's talk about something else.

OMAR: Dicho!

(After a very long silent pause.)

LIZ: What's tonight?

OMAR: Thursday night.

LIZ: Benny Moré night!

OMAR AND LIZ: CAFÉ NOSTALGIA!!

(Benny More's "Donde Estabas Tu" is heard. Liz and Omar get up and dance a cha-cha.)

The Architect, the Shrink and the Blind Man

SHRINK: And the thing that struck me the most is, I have never seen a city that's so fragmented. It's unbelievable! Everything is off on itself, and there's no sort of common strategic plan. No common theme.

And I'd have to say there's a lack of interest in what other people are doing. Everybody's focused on themselves and for their own area.

BLIND MAN: This is Lakeview Estates, and it's a mixture of many, many nationalities. There's a Haitian fellow who lives over there. There's a Greek who lives across the street. And another that way. You name it, we have it. Brazilians, Guatemalans, Salvadoreans, many nationalities.

ARCHITECT: As an architect, and second-generation Cubano, I feel Miami should be a place where all peoples and styles come together. I was in the Yucatán recently, and I saw people there that belong here: Mayas, Incas, Toltecs, Canadians . . .

SHRINK: Here they say there are three communities: the black community, the white community and the Hispanic community. Now, Hispanic, that sounded strange to me, Hispanic. That's a

language, right? What does that have to do with whether somebody comes from Costa Rica or Venezuela, for that matter? And it didn't take too long to figure out that people who spoke Spanish were pretty sensitive about it. For example, a person from Nicaragua doesn't want to associate with a person from Puerto Rico, or an Argentinean . . . well they don't want to be associated with anyone!

ARCHITECT: I am a Gusano, yet I don't share the vision or fanaticism of the right wing. I simply don't understand why I can't buy a ticket and go to Havana fuckin' tomorrow!

BLIND MAN: I am of Bahamian extraction. My parents came to this country in 1919. They had a very, very rough time. The way the Haitians are treated today was the way the Bahamians were treated when my parents came to this country.

ARCHITECT: I don't understand this country's treatment towards Haiti. Here in Miami, for instance, los Haitianos are treated like shit. Look man, they're an elegant people; they have something to offer me, I have something to offer them. I don't understand it, life, it seems is a series of unanswered questions.

SHRINK: And we have a black member on our staff. I mean he's black. I said "Look we're going to be meeting with some folks in the black community, maybe you ought to come with us?" He said, "Why me? What does this have to do with me?" I said, "Well you're black!"

He said, "No, I'm Haitian." Ha, see you can't pick a whole community and label them black. You can say the color of their skin is black. Then you got your black Cubans, but that's a black of a different color.

BLIND MAN: In years past it didn't matter whether you were from the Bahamas, Haiti or from the Dominican Republic, wherever, Barbados or Trinidad. If you were black, you were automatically labeled a Bahamian. And this was not true.

ARCHITECT: You know there was a time when you could drive your car down to the Keys, all the way down to Key West. You could take a ferry to Havana with your family, then you can take the same ferry to the Yucatán, and the next day come back to the Keys. Imagine driving your car around the Caribbean. From Havana to the Keys, an amazing gateway, but alas a sometimes military blockade!

SHRINK: Here in Miami, there's a lot of focus on status in a place where nobody has any status!

BLIND MAN: Do I have Anglo friends? In the '60s it was quite fashionable to have parties with my Anglo friends, as it was for my Anglo friends to throw parties with my black friends. This is not to say that I don't have Anglo friends. In fact some of my best friends are . . .

ARCHITECT: There is a map, drawn from the eyes of an outsider, much like yourselves. And in this map, you see Miami as an island, surrounded by water. The map is written in the language, the cartography of the eighteenth century. And in this map, you see, surrounded by water, a banana shape. And a million other islands. And the swamp, pantano! And the vegetation, tropical and baroque, and there's a rock outcropping, vez, and it recedes into the Everglades. And there's a slight rise, an elevation. And they built on this elevation, they fuckin' built Miami on this elevation! And this great event, Machiavellian in its own right, really. These side-by-side events, both tragic and necessary.

SHRINK: Horse shit! There's no history here. And there's a lot of focus on material things, a lot of emphasis on money, and you see this sort of display of all their material wealth.

BLIND MAN: Bahamian migrant workers came to this country here looking for a better life. An education for their children. And they said the Bahamians would work for a dollar and take the jobs away from the Americans, and that's what they said about the Cubans, and that's what they say today about the Haitians, and this is not true.

SHRINK: This place could really become a model city, there's a sense of hope here!

BLIND MAN: I never had the desire to leave Miami.

ARCHITECT: The medieval city crafted by hand and cut in stone.

SHRINK: Yeah, that one little word, hope.

ARCHITECT: Floating stones.

BLIND MAN: And by the same token, I have seen people make it here in Miami.

SHRINK: Here, people feel they can get a home, that they can advance.

BLIND MAN: And if they made it here, then I too can make it here.

ARCHITECT: Miami's a great fucking place!

SHRINK: My message to you is: don't be assholes, communicate!

BLIND MAN: I'm perfectly satisfied living in Miami.

ARCHITECT: I am very proud to be an American citizen.

(There is a long pause. The three freeze.

Radio static is heard. The blind man's cane tapping the floor is heard. The blind man, shrink and architect move slowly about the stage. The shrink stands behind the architect; the architect stands behind the blind man. The shrink and architect follow the blind man as they all slowly exit together. Lights fade to black.)

Since 1984, Culture Clash (Richard Montoya, Ric Salinas and Herbert Siguenza) has been storming the stages of such venues as the Kennedy Center, Lincoln Center, New York Shakespeare Festival/Public Theater, Mark Taper Forum, La Jolla Playhouse, INTAR Hispanic American Arts Center, Dallas Theater Center, Berkeley Repertory Theatre and South Coast Repertory, as well as countless university and community stages.

Culture Clash set a milestone for Latinos with thirty episodes of Fox TV's *Culture Clash*, the first Latino-themed sketch comedy television show to be executive produced and written by its stars. The show aired in seven markets in the United States. Culture Clash has appeared in the films *Encino Man* and *Hero*, and members of the group have been seen individually in *Falling Down, Mi Vida Loca* and *Star Maps*. In 1992, the group coproduced, wrote and starred in an award-winning short film entitled *Columbus on Trial*. That same year, their play *A Bowl of Beings* premiered on PBS's Great Performance series; their other works include *The Mission, S.O.S., Carpa Clash* and *Radio Mambo: Culture Clash Invades Miami*.

Culture Clash's future projects include two works which follow in the site-specific tradition of *Radio Mambo*. They are: *Culture Clash in Bordertown* (set in the San Diego/Tijuana region) and *Radio Manhattan*.